Outreach Programs for New Families

In  The Beginning

Having a Jewish Baby
and
Jewish Parenting Made Simple

Maggie Duwe, Editor
Dru Greenwood, Executive Editor

EXPERIMENTAL EDITION

A joint project of the UAHC-CCAR Commissions on Reform Jewish Outreach and
Synagogue Affiliation

Outreach Programs for New Families
In the Beginning...Having a Jewish Baby and
In the Beginning...Jewish Parenting Made Simple
is a joint project of the UAHC-CCAR Commissions on Reform Jewish Outreach and
Synagogue Affiliation.
Copyright 2001 by the Union of American Hebrew Congregations.

For further information about Outreach programming for Jewish or interfaith couples
raising Jewish children, contact the William and Lottie Daniel Department of Outreach,
633 Third Avenue, New York, NY 10017.
212.650.4230
outreach@uahc.org
synagogueaffiliation@uahc.org

Copyright © 2002, by the UAHC Press
Manufactured in the United States of America.

ISBN 0-8074-0811-5

0 1 2 3 4 5 6 7 8 9

"You have an opportunity to be part of the continuance of a remarkable tradition that is 4,000 years old but is yet so relevant and meaningful to modern times; you have an opportunity to know the fullness of the love, compassion and understanding that are an integral part of Judaism. You have an opportunity to be part of a unique religion, culture and community of people that emphasizes this world, rather than the next, that pursues social justice and freedom for all as part of the Jewish tradition of universalism."

David Belin, from *What Judaism Offers For You: A Reform Perspective*

"'Like gardens by the river's side' (*Numbers* 24:6). These are the teachers in Israel, who bring forth from our hearts wisdom, understanding and discernment, and teach us to do the will of God."

Tanna deBei Eliyahu, p. 116

"In the Beginning..." is dedicated with love and admiration to the memory
of

David Belin *z"l*

1928 – 1999

Chairman
UAHC-CCAR Commission on Reform Jewish Outreach
1978 - 1988

a true teacher in Israel, whose abundant love for Judaism and faith in Outreach inspired so many to seek a place for themselves in this remarkable tradition.

Acknowledgements

Many people contributed time and talent to the development of "In the Beginning… Having a Jewish Baby" and "In the Beginning…Jewish Parenting Made Simple." We are grateful to them all:

For imagining and fleshing out a new curriculum— Dr. Marcia Abraham, Debora Antonoff RJE, David Franklin, Fred Greene, Jennifer Jaech, Kathryn Kahn, Rob Nosanchuk, Rabbi Hara Person, and especially, Rabbi Michael Mayersohn, who gave of himself unstintingly and chaired the effort for the Commissions

For consultation on the role of the *mohel/et*— Dr. Dorothy Greenbaum, President of NOAM

For fruitful partnering among rabbis, early childhood educators and other staff in the six congregations that served as pilot sites, welcomed new families and helped to refine the curriculum—
- ♦ Rabbi Stephen Einstein and Roslin Romain of Congregation B'nai Tzedek, Fountain Valley, CA
- ♦ Rabbi Arnold Gluck and Eileen Kaplan of Temple Beth-El, Somerville, NJ
- ♦ Ava Harder, Regional Outreach Director, of the UAHC Northeast Council and Rabbi Jonah Pesner of Temple Israel, Boston
- ♦ Rabbi Shira Joseph, Rabbi Paula Goldberg and Beverly Goldberg of Shir Ami in Newtown, PA
- ♦ Rabbi Michael Mayersohn and Stella Haynes of Temple Beth David, Westminster, CA
- ♦ Rabbi James Prosnit and Gail Weinstein of B'nai Israel, Bridgeport, CT

For indispensable marketing and naming expertise— Milt Lieberman; for creative inspiration and ad design— Lisa Weinberger and her Masters Group Design staff; and for support in every aspect of producing this resource— Deborah Kirschner

For shepherding the pilot programs and accomplishing the massive task of compiling and editing the curriculum—all with good humor— Maggie Duwe

For their confidence in the worth of this project and for providing the needed support— Jerry and Roger Tilles

And, for all they taught us and will teach their children, we thank the couples whose eagerness to impart a Jewish heritage of depth and meaning to their children brought them to "In the Beginning."

In The Beginning

Table of Contents

Foreword

לְדוֹר וָדוֹר נַגִּיד גָּדְלֶךָ, וּלְנֵצַח נְצָחִים קְדֻשָּׁתְךָ נַקְדִּישׁ.

L'dor vador... "From generation to generation we will tell of Your greatness, and to all eternity we will sanctify Your holiness."

Jewish tradition holds that each new child born into the world comes with infinite potential. The chair of Elijah, herald of the Messiah, is readied for each Jewish baby as part of the *brit milah* or *brit chaim* ceremony. As a newborn is brought into the covenant, Jewish families pray for a life blessed with study of Torah, worthy of marital fulfillment and lifted up through loving deeds. Family and community gather to support new parents, rehearse the promise of blessing inherent in Jewish life, and welcome a new soul in Israel. The chain of generations, with one more added link, remains unbroken. Or does it?

Demographic trends today in North America mean that new parents are often isolated and unsure of the value that Judaism can bring to the life of their family. A Jewish mother and father may be distanced from their heritage by geography, years or circumstance. Intermarried, same-sex or single parents may wonder whether Judaism is accessible to or right for them. Searching for a way to express their own profound gratitude for the gift of life and to provide a stable framework of values for their children, many parents may not even know how to start.

The two programs in this resource have been designed to signal a warm welcome to all new families considering Judaism and to provide a place to begin. "In the Beginning... Having a Jewish Baby" is for expectant parents and "In the Beginning...Jewish Parenting Made Simple" is for parents of newborns and toddlers. Advertising through both formal and informal routes is a necessity. "Jewish Parenting Made Simple" provides babysitting and both programs are short and low-cost, all for easy accessibility. "In the Beginning..." also gives parents basic, immediately useable tools, from Jewish blessings and texts to deepen their own sense of meaning to board books, stuffed Torahs and phone numbers for the local Jewish pre-school for their children. The message to new families? "Reform Jews value and seek your participation in Jewish life. Reform Judaism has something of inestimable worth for you."

David Belin, *z''l*, in whose name "In the Beginning..." was developed, personified this message. From the early days of Outreach in 1978, when he chaired the Task Force on Reform Jewish Outreach, up to his untimely death in 1999, Mr. Belin directed his considerable genius and devotion to opening the doors of Jewish life to all seekers and to interfaith couples in particular. He saw possibilities for *keruv* (the mitzvah of drawing near those who are far) that eluded others and advocated tirelessly for fulfillment of the promise of Outreach. Everyone who works for Outreach and all whose lives have felt its impact will forever be in his debt. We are deeply grateful to Jerry and Roger Tilles for their generous funding of the "In the Beginning…" pilot programs in memory of David Belin.

Some of the responses of "In the Beginning…" pilot program participants begin to give voice to the fulfillment of the dream of Outreach:

- "We were so moved by this—moved to action about our Judaism, moved to tears sometimes when we discussed how welcome you have made us feel."
- "'In the Beginning…' gave us clues on how to create a healthy interfaith Jewish home."
- "Rituals have more significance now that we know the relevance of them."
- "I feel more connected with my religion and am looking forward to getting more serious about Judaism."
- "We would love to be part of ongoing events, for instance a reunion dinner with all our babies!"

Now it is our hope that Reform congregations everywhere will make use of this resource to create opportunities for Outreach and to welcome new families to partake in Jewish life from the outset. May our efforts be blessed with success from generation to generation.

Dr. Marcia Abraham, Chair   Barbara K. Shuman, Chair

Rabbi Stephen Einstein, Cochair   Rabbi Howard Jaffe, Cochair
Commission on Reform Jewish Outreach   *Commission on Synagogue Affiliation*

I.   INTRODUCTION

The 1990 National Jewish Population Survey, the authoritative demographic study of the American Jewish community conducted a decade ago, unequivocally demonstrated several facts with which synagogue leaders everywhere are all too familiar. Compared with earlier generations, Jews today are marrying later, intermarrying at an increasing rate, moving more frequently, having children later, and affiliating with synagogues later—often much later, when children reach religious school age. The combined impact of these trends, not likely to show any reversal in the much-anticipated 2000 NJPS, is troubling. Not only are congregations suffering from the absence of young adults and new families, but young adults and new families are losing the benefit of meaningful Jewish engagement for extended periods and at critical junctures in their lives.

The UAHC-CCAR Commissions on Reform Jewish Outreach and on Synagogue Affiliation, charged with responsibility for the Reform Movement's commitment to fulfilling the *mitzvah* of *keruv* (drawing near those who are far), have undertaken to meet this challenge in several ways. One critical effort is directed to new families, both to those expecting a child and to those with infants and toddlers.

> "Raise up a child in the way he should go, and he will never depart from it."
> *Proverbs* 22:6

It's never too soon to start. **"In the Beginning…Having a Jewish Baby"** and **"In the Beginning…Jewish Parenting Made Simple"** are gateway programs with liberal Jewish content designed to pique the interest of expectant and new parents who wish to understand Jewish rituals and traditions that will help them welcome and introduce their new child to Jewish life. "In the Beginning…" is designed for all parents either considering or planning to raise a Jewish child, including endogamous, intermarried, same gender and single parents, whether already affiliated with a synagogue or not. All are welcome.

As an Outreach program that builds on the success of "A Taste of Judaism: Are You Curious?", "In the Beginning…" is designed for easy accessibility. It's low cost, widely advertised, and short—only three sessions. Babysitting is provided. Each course covers three topics of special interest to new or expectant parents and helps parents gain tools that enable them to begin building a Jewish home with confidence. Rabbis and educators not only teach the sessions, but model the community's welcome and provide a personal link for next steps. From advertising and intake through interactive class sessions and multi-faceted follow up, "In the Beginning…" is designed to be the first step of many.

"IN THE BEGINNING..." GOALS

1. Convey a warm welcome on behalf of Reform Judaism to expectant parents and new families. It is not only possible, but beneficial, to find a place in a congregation.
2. Create a sense of sacred community among the participants. As they learn about Jewish life as it relates to their children, parents will be able to teach and support one another.
3. Provide information about Jewish texts and traditions that relate to childbirth and/or parenting. Demonstrate that practicing Judaism can greatly enhance family life, support good parenting and help children develop strong values. Demystify Jewish rituals and provide tools so each participant can make informed choices.
4. Whet the appetite for further activity. Encourage participants to seek additional classes and options for participation within the Jewish community.

PROGRAM FORMAT

"In the Beginning..." meets once a week for two-hour sessions in three consecutive weeks. Classes are kept small to allow for discussion and for the development of community. (Ideal class size is five to eight couples.) The special needs of expectant parents and new parents for comfort, healthy snacks and appropriate meeting times must be honored. Consider meeting in a youth lounge with comfortable chairs or in the synagogue library. Provide decaffeinated beverages and fruit and cookies or bagels and cream cheese. Provide a babysitting option in a nearby room for parents or expectant parents with small children. Consider meeting on a Sunday afternoon or early evening, particularly to accommodate young families.

Fees

Program fees should be set to cover the minimal direct costs of the program while remaining low enough to encourage participation. (Consider a range of $36 to $50.)

"IN THE BEGINNING..." PARTICIPANTS

As indicated above, depending on the program you choose to offer, all expectant or all new parents are welcome. Particularly in the case of expectant parents, who after all are only expecting for about nine months, it's important to gather a large enough group at one time to make "Having a Jewish Baby" viable. Concerns about combining interfaith parents and endogamous Jewish parents in the same group have proved unfounded. Although some issues are different, the differences are overwhelmed by the common need to start at the beginning. Couples with two Jewish partners are able to assure interfaith couples that they are indeed welcome and, in fact, share similar concerns. In one "Jewish Parenting Made Simple" class, Jewish parents particularly expressed appreciation for the questions asked by the interfaith couples. Those questions had led to deeper thoughtfulness for the Jewish parents.

One pilot program, titled "In the Beginning…And Baby Makes Three," was open only to interfaith couples and included both expectant and new parents. This variation also worked well.

ADMINISTRATORS AND TEACHERS

Choose an administrator or program coordinator who enjoys meeting and engaging people both on the phone and in person. The coordinator will be responsible for registration, answering any and all questions about the program, alleviating concerns, welcoming couples and following up.

Excellent teachers are essential to the success of any program and "In the Beginning…" is no exception. The pilot programs were all taught either by the congregation's rabbi or by the rabbi and early childhood specialist or Outreach director together. (While the latter pattern is obviously an intensive commitment of staff, it proved a powerful combination for effective programming, providing male/female role modeling, a consistent balance of content and process strengths, and a clear message about the congregation's commitment to Outreach to new families. Couples gained familiarity not only with the rabbi, but also with another key professional with whom they would be likely to interact regularly as a family with a young child.) As models, teachers must be well-rooted in their knowledge and practice of Judaism and invest their teaching with their passion for Jewish life. Because "In the Beginning…" is designed for a diverse and tentative population, teachers must be prepared to respond to the inevitably challenging questions in an open and honest manner.

II. PROGRAM ESSENTIALS

MARKETING AND PUBLICITY

When planning your marketing strategy, more is more, and more is better. By all means, use the synagogue's usual means of getting the word out: bulletin articles, announcements on your website and from the *bimah*, flyers sent home with religious school and nursery children, posters, postcards stamped with "pass this along to a friend," etc. One pilot site of five registered the majority of participants through internal publicity.

However, the predominant response for "In the Beginning..." pilot programs came from advertising in major secular newspapers. The characteristics of the population for this Outreach program, like others, mean that they are not likely to be reached through regular synagogue routes. They are probably not members and won't see the bulletin or hear the announcement from the *bimah*. They may be new to town. They may assume that they're not welcome, particularly if they are intermarried, single, or gay or lesbian. So use the major secular paper that most of your congregants read and place the ad in the feature or news section of the paper. Budget accordingly. Though pilot programs did have a minimal response from smaller local newspapers, these did not prove to be cost effective.   News releases and feature articles carry no fee. They can also be developed and marketed to your local newspapers. (See examples of ads, news releases and articles following each curriculum.)

Publicity Recommendations for Program Administrator

- Ask rabbis, educators and temple administrators which newspapers are read most frequently by congregants and which papers cover most of the geographical area you want to reach. Major city newspapers are significantly more effective than local town papers. (That's why their advertising rates are higher!)
- Are there Expectant Parents or Baby magazines? Is there a weekly geared for people in their twenties or thirties?
- Develop a relationship with an ad executive at each newspaper and ask the following questions:
  - Which day does each newspaper have the largest circulation? Are there any "add-ons" if you target certain days of the week? One paper in the pilot program included a free mailer to all "Sunday only" subscribers when a Friday ad was purchased.
  - Discuss placement of ads, eg. main news section versus entertainment section versus "lifestyle". Be specific about where you want the ad to be placed. Avoid the religion section.
  - Is there a non-profit rate? Or a religious rate?
  - Is there a discount for two or more ads run in the same week? Or for three consecutive weeks?
  - Are there regional sections that target a specific part of the city? (Rates for specific zones are much lower than for the total circulation and may better reach your target audience.)

- In order to have enough turn around time for registration, ads must begin running four to five weeks prior to the starting date of the class. If possible, these ads should appear twice per week for three or four consecutive weeks.
- Mail or fax a copy of the "In the Beginning…" ad to your contact person at the newspaper. Be sure to do this well in advance and ask to see a proof copy of what will appear. Check the copy carefully before approving it.
- Check the ad every time it appears to make sure it is being run as agreed: size, section, frequency, etc. If an error is made, request an additional ad run.
- Publicity releases: Press releases are a useful way to give further details about these classes and are free as a service to the local readership. Each newspaper has a preferred format that you must use in order for the press release to be readily accepted. Send press releases (and a photo if you have one) to all local town newspapers.

INTAKE AND REGISTRATION

The **intake call** is the first contact with a prospective participant and sets the tone for the whole interaction. Although some callers will be excited about the program and eager to sign up, others may seem tentative. They may be unsure if the class is appropriate for them and wonder if they will be welcome. The **intake person** must be reassuring and ready to provide full information about the program. A warm, understanding manner when answering the phone is essential.

Profile of Callers and Possible Concerns
Jews:
- If they are intermarried, they may fear rejection despite the wording in the ad.
- Often they remember their religious training in a negative way and are hesitant to try again.
- Judaism is important to them, but they have a hard time explaining why, particularly to partners who are not Jewish.
- They may not have had contact with the Jewish community in years. They may feel guilty about this and embarrassed about their ignorance of their tradition.

Non-Jews:
- This may be their first contact with a Jewish institution and they don't know what to expect.
- They are intermarried and not sure how to raise their children or even if they themselves will be welcome.
- Some may be considering conversion, but are not ready to make that decision.
- They are open and excited about new information, but not sure how their relationship with their own parents may be affected.

Intake as resource for instructors
The intake call and registration forms provide a vital source of information for the class instructor. One of the goals of this program is to establish Jewish connections. Since the class only meets three times, it is very helpful for the teacher to begin with as much understanding of her/his students' background and needs as possible. *Take time to write*

down callers' stories and feelings on the intake form. (See sample intake and registration forms in the section on each program.)

To assure a good connection with the caller, begin by asking what the goals of the couple are in taking this class. Why are they interested in taking this class at this time? Congratulate the caller on the expected birth or on the new baby. Make copies of all intake and registration forms and send them to the teacher a week before the class begins.

Information for administrator

In addition to the particulars of time, place, cost, babysitting, etc., administrators need to know the goals of the program. "In the Beginning…" is designed to:
1. Help expectant and new parents welcome their baby into the richness and beauty of Judaism through ritual and tradition.
2. Give expectant parents a face to face experience with a *mohel* and with birth ceremonies for their daughters and give new parents tools for Jewish parenting, such as blessings, bedtime and Shabbat rituals.
3. Introduce new Jewish parents to one another and to the Jewish community.
4. Give parents ideas and introductions for further Jewish learning, if desired.

The following procedures will ease registration and assure that participants feel welcome.
- Explain to the caller that classes fill up quickly. Encourage them to fill out and mail their registration form as soon as possible to insure their spot in the class. ONLY after the registration is returned, with payment, are they enrolled in the class.
- After filling out the intake form, send the registration form and directions to the caller.
- Make copies of all intake and registration forms and send them to the instructor along with an attendance sheet.
- Keep names, addresses, phone numbers and e-mail addresses for follow-up.

GENERAL TIPS

To facilitate a more intimate environment and promote the feeling of community:
1. Set up chairs in a circle or around a table
2. Provide name tags
3. Provide appropriate refreshments
4. Provide babysitting option
5. Prepare handouts
6. Prepare a name and address list of participants to distribute the first session (if participants agree). Include contact numbers and addresses of the teacher, the administrator and the synagogue.

FOLLOW-UP

Follow-up and evaluation are *essential* components of this Outreach program. No matter how wonderful the program itself, without follow-up the goals of "In the Beginning…" cannot be met. Coming to this program may be the first step toward Jewish life, the first time in recent memory to meet a rabbi or educator, the first tentative exploration of a synagogue or a Jewish preschool. A majority of the participants in the pilot programs expressed the desire to continue Jewish study and Jewish community connection. By keeping graduates of "In the Beginning" informed of Jewish community activities, you can assure that this will be the first of many Jewish connections for them.

Suggestions
1. The mailing list must be complete and accurate.
2. Follow up with each participant in a timely manner according to the needs expressed on the Evaluation Form. Be sure to inform your membership or Outreach chair of participants' interest.
3. If possible, when scheduling "In the Beginning…," make sure that other programs of potential interest will be available following the program. Interfaith couples programs, Introduction to Judaism, and other adult education classes may be of particular interest. It is important to supply this information.
4. Keep participants informed of local and regional Outreach activities.
5. Put participants on your synagogue mailing list to receive the bulletin.
6. Consider a reduced synagogue membership rate for one year for "In the Beginning…" graduates or offer them other special opportunities, such as an invitation to the congregational Seder, High Holiday tickets, a special invitation to Tot Shabbat or a Sukkah celebration. Be sure to acknowledge their presence on these occasions and introduce them to other congregants.
7. Provide a reduced-rate coupon for "Mommy and Me" or another infant/toddler program.
8. Schedule a special reunion Shabbat dinner or Havdalah celebration.

III.   CURRICULUM FOR "IN THE BEGINNING...HAVING A JEWISH BABY"

A note to teachers: The curriculum plans outlined here have been developed, piloted and edited with the goals of "In the Beginning..." in mind and with the hope that those who use them in the future will further adapt them to individual teaching styles and to the needs of particular program participants. "In the Beginning..." shares an approach similar to that of "A Taste of Judaism: Are You Curious?" Imparting complete information on what Judaism says about a given topic is *not* the aim of the program; conveying a sense of enthusiasm and excitement about the possibilities of Jewish life and assurance that it is possible to grow into it, with some sweet, compelling and relevant examples for practice and mastery along the way, *is* the aim of the program. Use traditional and modern Jewish texts as a touchstone for meaning and encourage dialogue within and among couples. Assume that your students are sophisticated adult beginners who want to learn and to be the best parents that they can be. Connect with your students and teach to your passion. Feel free to adjust the curriculum accordingly.

Suggested common rubrics for each class session:
1. Set the tone for each class by writing a short quote to pique interest on a flipchart or blackboard. Suggestions are provided.
2. Introduce the idea of "car talk" at the end of the first session. Ask couples to take note of their discussion on the way home from each session. What most stuck with them from the session? What questions arose for them? Begin each subsequent session with a short discussion of car talk to refocus the group and pick up loose ends from the previous session.
3. Provide break time with refreshments and access to facilities for couples to talk informally.
4. Prepare handouts and lists of resources for couples to take home.

In
The Beginning

"In the Beginning...Having a Jewish Baby"

Session 1: Blessings—a bridge to respond to God

Materials needed:

> Class list with names and addresses
> Copies of the *Shehecheyanu* (Hebrew, transliteration and English)
>> See Blessings sheets on p. 48-49, which should be laminated.
> Copies of any texts you plan to study (see below)
> Multiple copies of the traditional *brachah* preface (Hebrew, transliteration and English)

Prior to class write on board:
"Each child brings its own blessing into the world."

Jewish Folk Saying

- Begin with welcome and introduction of teacher.
  Explain the Reform Movement's commitment to Outreach and interest in this particular program.
  Tell why you are excited about teaching this class.
  Also, explain that there will be a short saying posted every week, just as an entrée to the week's session.

- Review the goals of the program and today's session:
  - To give some tools and practical information for a Jewish beginning, which all are about to experience.
  - To begin to notice the miracles in our everyday lives and make them more special with a blessing.
  - To strengthen the bonds within your new family and families of origin.
  - To create a sense of community within the group. Hopefully, participants will begin to see each other as a support team.
  - To strengthen your connection with the synagogue and the Jewish community. "We want you to know you are welcome and we are glad you are here."

- Invite participants to introduce themselves and speak briefly about why they are taking this class now. Note that we all hope for a healthy child and a safe delivery and ask each person to share one special dream he/she has for the anticipated child.

- Introduce the *Shehecheyanu*:
  - a blessing recited to signify something new in our lives or to mark happy occasions
  - can be recited when eating a strawberry for the first time this year, buying a new house, or seeing your baby's first smile.
  - could also be recited in the delivery room or when you are alone as a family for the first time.

Distribute a handout of Hebrew, transliteration, and English. Ask participants to bring it each week. Teach the meaning of the words and why it is an appropriate blessing now as this class begins. Say the blessing.

- Retell or ask a participant to read the text from *The Book of Legends,* (p. 311, section 638 -2nd paragraph).

  Explain *aggadah,* a wonderful way the ancient Rabbis had of teaching and explaining their thoughts and other texts through stories. Note that all are about to be blessed with a new human being in their lives. ("As a friend of mine said at the birth of their son, 'there were five people in the room and then…there were six.'") This is a time full of wonder. Discuss:
  - What are the attributes of you and your partner that you hope will bless your child? Example: My partner can see the positive in situations. Or I enjoy being in the backyard with my plants. These are things for which we could write blessings.
- Introduce the concept of "blessings."
  - Why do Jews bless? We are partners with God when we bless. Blessings are a bridge enabling us to respond to God.
  - Blessings can be for each other, for a house, for a safe trip, and for the everyday routine. One of the wonderful things about Judaism is its way of taking notice of special occasions and even of everyday occurrences and making them special. One of our jobs as Jews is to notice the everyday miracles. Distribute and/or read examples of traditional and modern blessings. (Choose examples, including blessings for children, from *Gates of Prayer, Kol Haneshamah,* or *The Book of Blessings* by Marcia Falk.) Read and discuss differences in style, language and tone. Some are more traditional; others simpler and more direct. What they all have in common is a way to acknowledge sacred moments.
  - How can participants make this time of expectancy a blessing for themselves as individuals and as a couple? For their families, including their own parents? How can they be inclusive of family from a different religion?
- Teach the what, where, why, and how of blessings.
  - Explain the customary components and language of a traditional Jewish blessing.
  - Hand out sheets with the *brachah* preface in Hebrew, transliteration, and English.
  - "*Baruch atah Adonai….*" This is the "yeah God" part with a particular value attached.
  - Altogether, a *brachah* provides a window into a primary Jewish value: to honor life in all its richness and complexity.
  - Since Hebrew is the Jewish language, the goal is to say the blessings in Hebrew. But God understands all languages. The important thing is to raise everyday moments to the level of special, to notice the sacred in the dailyness of life. A *brachah* is an entree into all of Jewish liturgy and life.
  - Invite each person individually to write a blessing for his/her baby. Begin with the traditional Hebrew, "*Baruch Atah…,* and then finish it in English.

- Invite each person individually to write a blessing for his/her baby. Begin with the traditional Hebrew, "*Baruch Atah...*, and then finish it in English. What are your hopes and dreams for this child? What do you wish for her/him more than anything else? When individuals have finished writing, ask couples to combine their individual blessings into one.

—Take a break—

- Ask for volunteers to share their blessings with the group. Discuss:
  - How did it feel to bless your baby in this way?
  - When could you use your blessing? (as part of your birth announcement?)
  - Encourage participants to try writing a blessing for their partner during the coming week. Remind them that this is a way to notice the everyday things that you wish to lift to the level of a sacred moment. Don't aim for "the perfect" blessing, but simply say to yourself or share how you feel when you see your partner smile at you, for example.

Suggest that the group as a whole write a blessing for itself. Write it on the board and record it to bring back during the last session.

- Review and extend the discussion of blessings.
  - Did these blessings feel like they could be sacred moments? Life is full of such times. What about a blessing for the first time you see your child? Try writing that this week, as well.
  - Are there times when a blessing could <u>create</u> a sacred moment? ("Do you think that, if you said a quiet blessing such as the *shehecheyanu* the first time you ate a tomato this summer, it would taste better? Would it taste more like a gift from God? Or would you feel you are making a very sacred moment even more so by having your *chuppah*, if you had one, over the bed in which your child is born? An alternative might be a quilt that belongs to your parents or even grandparents.)
  - Suggest that participants pay attention to the sacred moments in the week ahead and think of short blessings, including the *shehecheyanu,* to mark them. (Good practice for the time their baby smiles for the first time—a blessing will be ready on their lips.)
- Closing.
  - Thank participants for their openness and willingness to take risks. (This was a good prelude to childbirth!)
  - Introduce "car talk."
  - Express your eagerness to see them again next week and announce the topic: covenant and ceremonies of welcome. A *mohel/et* will meet with them and answer questions.

In  The Beginning

Session 2: Covenant—ceremonies for welcoming your baby

Materials needed:

    Extra class lists with names and addresses

    Additional copies of the *Shehecheyanu* (Hebrew, transliteration and English)

    Copies of the *Tanakh* or of particular texts you plan to study (see below)

    Copies of sample *brit milah* ceremony

    Handout outlining the rubrics of the *brit milah* ceremony

Prior to class write on board:

"Honor your father and mother, even as you honor God; for all three were partners in your creation." *The Zohar* (Define)

- Welcome back! (Take attendance.)
  - Did anyone find him/herself saying blessings this week?
  - Did you notice sacred moments that deserved a blessing?
  - Anything special come up in "car talk"?
- Review the *Shehecheyanu*. Note that this *brachah* is said when friends see each other after a time apart, so it's appropriate for this occasion.
- Introduce the session topics: *brit milah*, covenant, what it means for a child to be Jewish, meeting with a *mohel/et*. (Next week—the final session—will include birth ceremonies for daughters and Jewish names and naming traditions.)
- Ask participants what they know about a "*bris*" or *Brit Milah*.
  - What is it? (Write participants' ideas on the board. Responses will likely include what participants know about the ceremony.) Note that the *mohel/et* will describe the ceremony and procedures in detail and answer questions in a few minutes. First look at the meaning behind *bris* or *brit* as the "covenant of circumcision." (Explain varied pronunciations.)
  - What is a covenant? (Possible responses: agreement between two parties that has expectations and rewards included; more than a legal contract, "covenant" implies a sacred dimension, the presence of God). Note that the idea of a covenant connection between God and the Jewish people is central to Judaism and Jewish life.
- Review Biblical texts about covenant—3 of them in the Torah, all of which remain in effect today. (One doesn't supercede the other.) Questions to address: Who are parties to this *brit*? What are the terms of the *brit*? What is expected of each party? What is the sign of the *brit*? (This can be done as a group of the whole, or as a small group activity, debriefed together.)
  - *Genesis* 9:8-17
    Covenant that God makes with Noah never to send a flood again, utterly destroying the world. Note that this *brit* or covenant does not include circumcision. All humankind is included in Noah's *brit*. Rainbow is a universal sign.
  - *Genesis* 15:18-21, *Genesis* 17:9-16 and 21.
    Covenant that God makes with Abraham. Note what is promised and what demanded. Why circumcision? Individual mark of the covenant. What is Sarah's role in the covenant? Because she is included, we can

infer that it is equally important to bless and have a ceremony welcoming our daughters into the covenant. Gender equality is a key element in Reform Judaism.

- *Exodus* 31:16-18 and *Exodus* 19:5-8. Note that these are part of the full encounter with God at Sinai, excerpts that particularly address *brit*. Covenant that God makes with the Israelites through Moses. In the first excerpt Shabbat is promised and demanded and also the sign of Israel's covenant. The tablets (Torah) are also a sign. In the second excerpt Israel (as one people) is expected to obey and in turn is promised to be God's holy people.
- *Deuteronomy* 29:9-14. Note who is included in the *brit* that Moses reiterates at the very end of his life—future generations and proselytes.

—Take a Break—

- Welcoming all newcomers, girls and boys equally, into the *brit* is obviously of great importance. This session will address *brit milah* (for boys) and the next session will address *brit banot* (for girls.)
  Introduce the *mohel/et*.
  *Note to instructor: If possible, invite a *mohel/et* certified by the Berit Mila Board of Reform Judaism. These *mohalim/ot* are Jewish physicians and other health professionals who are specially trained not only in the medical practice of circumcision and the religious aspects of *brit milah*, but also in the sociology of contemporary American Jewish families and the Reform mandate for Outreach to unaffiliated and interfaith couples. For information about Reform *mohalim/ot* nearby, go to http://www.rj.org/beritmila/index.html and click on the current list of practicing *mohalim/ot* listed by state or province. Whether you use a Reform *mohel/et* or not, the *mohel/et* should be someone local who works frequently with you or your congregation. He or she should be knowledgeable about the Reform position on patrilineal descent and sensitive to the additional family issues raised by intermarriage or conversion at the time of a *bris*. Suggest that the *mohel/et* bring copies of a sample ceremony or provide one yourself.
  Topics to include:
  - "who"—*mohel/et* or doctor and what his/her training has been, as well as the role of a *mohel/et*.
  - "what"—the details of what happens during a usual ceremony of *brit milah*. Reference to a sample ceremony will be useful here. What are the roles family members will play? What are the medical considerations for proceeding with a *brit milah*, for the baby's comfort during the circumcision, and for aftercare? What are the elements of a *bris* (refer to handout) and why is each included? How can the experience be enhanced and the *mitzvah* celebrated?
  - "where"—the pros and cons of home, synagogue or hospital.
  - "when"—early on the eighth day, even on Yom Kippur, unless the baby's health is in question.

13

- "how"—public or private, how arrangements should be made. Emphasize that some parts of the ceremony are dictated by tradition, but that other parts allow for a great deal of variation and family creativity.
  Allow plenty of time for questions and answers.
- Refer back to the earlier discussion of *brit* (covenant). "What is the covenant between parent and child? Child and parent?" How does Judaism see this relationship?
  - Write on board: "You shall each revere his mother and his father, and keep My Sabbaths: I the Lord am your God." (Leviticus 19:3) What does that mean?
  - Write on board under the above text: "My message to parents is: Every day ask yourselves the question: 'What is there about me that deserves the reverence of my child?'" Abraham Joshua Heschel
  - How does it feel to be part of a Covenant of a people with God? with your coming child, and with each other? Try writing a letter describing a Covenant for your family even before your child is born, including your hopes for and responsibilities to your child and each other.
- *L'hitraot.* Remind participants about car talk. Announce next week's topic and note that it will be the last session.

In 🎲🎲🎲
The Beginning

Session 3: Jewish naming—creating a Jewish environment for your baby
Materials needed:

Extra class lists with names and addresses
Additional copies of the laminated Blessings sheet, including *Shehecheyanu*
        (in Hebrew, transliteration and English)
Copies of the *Tanakh* or of particular texts you plan to study (see below)
Copies of sample *brit bat* ceremonies (See Appendix.)
Extra handouts outlining the rubrics of the *brit milah* ceremony
Hebrew and English naming books
Shabbat blessings for children in Hebrew, transliteration and English
Evaluation forms
Bibliography
Community Resource List, including other UAHC Outreach programs such as
        Introduction to Judaism
(Optional) Special gift for the new family, e.g. half-price coupon for "Mommy
and Me," stuffed Torah or Jewish board book, UAHC "Bedtime Rituals"
pamphlet, or   Jewish lullaby tape

Prior to class write on board:
"Every person has three names: one given by his father and mother, one others call him,
and one he earns himself."
Ecclesiastes Rabbah 7: 1. (Define *midrash.*)

- Begin with *shehecheyanu.*
- Welcome back! (Take attendance.)
  - Anything special come up in "car talk"?
  - Refer back to Covenant and invite participants to share letters expressing a
    covenant for their family.
- Note that this is the final session and introduce the session topics: *brit bat,* Jewish
  names and naming traditions, and creating a Jewish environment for your child.
- *Brit Bat.* Remind participants that welcoming *all* newcomers, girls and boys
  equally, into the *brit* is of central importance in Judaism. Set the context in which
  Reform Judaism encourages welcoming ceremonies for girls and boys, each
  having equal importance. While the sign of Abraham's covenant is circumcision
  and thus only applies to males, there is ample latitude in Jewish tradition for
  developing rituals of entry into the covenant for girls and for creating meaningful
  ceremonies to surround the covenantal moment for both girls and boys. Note that
  Judaism has always adapted to the circumstances and needs of different times and
  places; Reform Judaism follows in that tradition. In this day, we consider it a
  mitzvah to enter a daughter into the Covenant, because we consider females, like
  males, to be full inheritors of the Covenant.
  - Historically and in Orthodox synagogues today, the "welcoming" of a baby
    girl includes the father being called up to the Torah for an *aliyah,* a blessing
    for the health of the mother, and announcement of the girl's Hebrew name.
    Usually mother and daughter were not present. What other options are there if
    you have a daughter?

- As you'll see in the sample ceremonies for girls, Reform rabbis involved in developing these rituals have drawn on three alternate themes related to *brit*: light, Torah, and *tallit* (the fringes that remind a Jew every day of God's demands for fulfilling the *brit* at Sinai). In light of these possible themes, they constructed three possible rituals:
    - lighting seven candles for the seven days of Creation culminating in Shabbat,
    - lifting the baby to touch her hands to the Torah, and
    - wrapping her in a *tallit*.
- Though the title of these ceremonies is not set, it is important that the word *Brit* be included to indicate its covenantal nature. *Brit Chaim* (life), *Brit Bat* (daughter), *Brit Banot* (daughters), and *Brit Rehitzah* are examples.
- Recall learning about blessings in the first session. Making this moment sacred requires a *brachah*. Examples:
    - *Baruch ata Adonai, Eloheinu Melech ha-olam, asher b'chocho anu madlikin ner shel simcha v'chayyim.* Blessed are You, Oh God, Creator of the Universe, by whose power we kindle the lights of happiness and of life. (Rabbi William Dreskin)
    - *Baruch ata Adonai, Eoheinu Melech ha-olam, asher kidshanu b'mitzvotav v'tzivanu l'hachnasah b'v'rit hachayim.* We praise You, Eternal our God, Sovereign of the universe. You hallow us with Your *mitzvot*, and command us to bring our daughters into the Covenant of Life. (Stern, *On the Doorposts of Your House*)
- Read *Malachi* 3:1. Elijah is known as the "angel of the Covenant" and the one who will herald the Messiah or the Messianic Age. (Remind participants of Elijah's role at *Pesach* and at the end of *Havdalah*.) A special chair for Elijah invokes the presence of the prophet, angel, and protector at a *bris*. Since we hold that every child has unlimited potential—can bring the Messianic Age, so Elijah's chair should be present for girls as well as for boys. Decorate a chair to be used by an honored guest holding the baby during part of the ceremony.
- Review samples of *Brit Bat* ceremonies. (Choose among samples in this resource, as well as those in the following publications: *On the Doorposts of Your House*, pgs.116-120; *Lifecycles*, Vol. I, p. 53-82; *How to Be a Jewish Parent,* pgs. 168-172, and *The New Jewish Baby Book*, 147-169.)
- Introduce examples of ways to enhance the chosen ritual:
    1. Form two lines of guests holding lighted candles and bring the baby in through the line of lights.
    2. Hold up the baby with both hands on the Torah and recite the text from Psalms 119:48.
    3. Place the baby in the center of a *tallit* held at the four corners by parents and honored guests; fold the *tallit* over the baby and recite Psalms 36:8, 104:1 and 30, 91:1-4, and/or 121:5, 7, 8.
    4. Alternatively or additionally, parents, baby and other siblings stand wrapped in a *tallit*. (This *tallit* could later be used at the girl's Bat Mitzvah. As a sign of continuity from generation to generation, the

16

grandparents could recite the same verses from Psalms at the Bat Mitzvah.)

5. Foot washing is symbolic of status as an honored guest, recalling Abraham's welcome of the three angels who announced Isaac's birth (*Genesis* 18:2-5).

6. Any of these ceremonies could be ended with the following text, loosely translated from *Malachi* 2:5. "God makes a Covenant with her; a Covenant of life and peace."

- Review options for scheduling: *Rosh Chodesh*, already known as a women's time; eight days following the birth, corresponding with the timing for *Brit Milah*; Shabbat immediately following the birth, corresponding with the traditional time for naming girls in synagogue (may be too soon for the mother). As yet, there is no *halachah* on this matter. Any time between the eighth and thirty-first day is possible, but, unless health issues intervene, preferably not later.

—Take a Break—

- *Naming.* A major element of either a *brit milah* or a *brit bat* is giving the newborn a name. So let's turn to Jewish naming traditions and the way Jewish values are passed from generation to generation through a name. A name reflects who we want our child to be. Names can be an expression of individuality, recall a great life event, serve as a tribute to someone deceased, or an honor to someone living.
  - Discussion: How did you get your name? Do you have a Hebrew name? How did you get it? Do you think a name makes a difference in a person's life? Note that in the Torah no two people have the same name, making names and their uniqueness very important.
  - What does the Torah have to say about naming?
    - Read *Genesis* 2:19-20. What does this text say about the importance of naming?
    - Read *Genesis Rabbah*, XVII, 4. Review the meaning of *midrash* and ask how this text amplifies the meaning of the *Genesis* text. (Adam, even over the "ministering Angels," is given the honor of naming the animals, and indeed naming God and himself.)
    - Read *Isaiah* 42:8 and *Exodus* 3:13-15. What does the Torah say about the importance of God's name to God?
    - Read *Genesis* 32:23-31. What is the significance of Jacob's name becoming Israel?
    - Read *Genesis* 17:1-10 and 15-16. What is the significance of Abram and Sarai becoming Abraham and Sarah? Note that the *heh* added to each of their names is part of God's name.
  - Explain the form of a Jewish name (*Ploni ben Ploni v'Plonah)*, constructed to indicate the relationship of generations, and when it's used (for an *aliyah*, on a *ketubah*, etc.). Some rabbis will not include the name of a parent of another religion. Others think it important and include the English name of that parent.

17

For Jews-by-choice the names Abraham and Sarah are traditionally used as the names of their Jewish "parents."

- Describe various naming traditions (*minhag* of different communities):
  - Match the first letter of the name of someone you want to honor (eg. Simon might be a name chosen to honor grandpa Sam),
  - Choose a name for its literal meaning,
  - Emulate the fine personal qualities of a Biblical character or a relative. Give examples and refer participants to the name books.
  - Naming can also be for a deceased relative, an Ashkenazic tradition. It doesn't have to be the exact name. For instance, *Miriam's Well* tells the story about parents who wanted to name their daughter after her deceased grandmother, whose name, in Yiddish, was Faige, which means bird. In English it was Frances. The mother couldn't name her daughter Frances, because "it just felt too close." So, she took the "f" and "r" from Frances. These became the *peh* and *resh* in the daughter's first name Tiferet. Then her middle name, Sassona, meaning joy or delight, was formed from the last four letters of Frances. And now her mother will always be present in the name of her child. It doesn't have to be as complicated as this though. A friend's son is named for his great grandmother. Her name was Bessie and his is Benjamin.
  - Over the years names have also been adapted to the current time. Moses was an Egyptian name and Esther was Babylonian.
  - Ask if anyone knows any other Jewish naming customs.
- Discussion: How do you feel about naming your baby? What do you want to accomplish for your child by the name you choose? Are you going to name your child after someone? Who? Why? Why not?
- *Transmitting Jewish Identity.* Discussion: Names are important because of what they represent about the values you wish to pass on to your child from past generations. However, Jewish identity and meaning cannot be transmitted simply through a name. How can participants begin actually to transmit identity to a child once he/she is born? How is a Jewish environment created? (It's never too early!) Elicit suggestions and fill in, also indicating that of course the answer to this question will take a lifetime to answer. Suggestions might include
  - i. Jewish symbols (Hebrew name on child's door or pillow)
  - ii. mezuzah at child level
  - iii. Jewish art
  - iv. Jewish story books
  - v. Jewish smells such as challah baking
  - vi. Jewish music
  - vii. Shabbat celebrations.
- *Feedback and closing.* You are now 3 weeks closer to the birth of your baby than you were when we started. Remember, as you experience this time of your lives, you have a support team. You have your generations of family, friends, Jewish community and synagogue, and now you have your friends from this group.
  - Distribute evaluation forms and allow a few minutes for participants to fill them out. (**Collect them before participants leave.**)

- Write the group blessing, from the first session, on the board. Ask what might have changed since the first session.
- What will you take with you from our three weeks together? Has "In the Beginning…" influenced the way you will welcome your baby? What have we done to help you prepare?
- Distribute gifts and handouts for follow-up.

Mazal tov! Have a happy healthy Jewish baby! Keep in touch with us.

In בראשית
The Beginning

RESOURCES FOR "HAVING A JEWISH BABY"

1. Abramowitz, Yosef I., and Silverman, Susan. *Jewish and Family Life*. Golden Books, 1997.
2. Bialik, Hayim Nahman, and Ravnitzky, Yehoshua Hana, ed. *The Book of Legends*. Schocken Books, 1992.
3. Diamant, Anita with Kushner, Karen. *How to be a Jewish Parent-A Practical Handbook for Family Life*. Schocken Books, 2000.
4. Diamant, Anita. *The New Jewish Baby Book*. Jewish Lights Publishing, 1993.
5. Falk, Marcia. *The Book of Blessings*. Beacon Press, 1996.
6. *Gates of Prayer*. Central Conference of American Rabbis, 1975.
7. Gribetz, Jessica. *Wise Words, Jewish Thoughts, and Stories Through the Ages*. William Morrow & Co., 1997.
8. *On the Doorposts of Your House*, Central Conference of American Rabbis, 1994.
9. Orenstein, Debra, ed. *Lifecycles: Jewish Women on Life Passages and Personal Milestones, Vol. 1.* Jewish Lights Publishing, 1994.
10. Rosten, Leo. *Treasury of Jewish Quotations*. Bantam Books, 1972.
11. Reuben, Steven Carr. *Raising Jewish Children in a Contemporary World*. Prima Publishing, 1992.
12. *Tanakh, JPS Hebrew-English*, The Jewish Publication Society, 1999.

RESOURCE SHEETS—"In the Beginning...Having a Jewish Baby"

Session 1-1
Blessings--*Brachot*

1. בָּרוּךְ אַתָּה, יְיָ אֱלֹהֵינוּ, מֶלֶךְ הָעוֹלָם, שֶׁהֶחֱיָנוּ וְקִיְּמָנוּ
וְהִגִּיעָנוּ לַזְּמַן הַזֶּה.

Ba-ruch a-ta Adonai, Eh-lo-hei-nu Meh-lech ha-o-lam sheh-heh-cheh-ya-nu v'ki-y'manu, v'higi-anu la'z'man ha'zeh.

We praise You, Eternal God, Sovereign of the Universe, for giving us life, for sustaining us, and for enabling us to reach this season.

2. When to say *shehecheyanu*: Upon eating your first strawberry of spring.
At the birth of a child. / When your baby says "Mama" or "Papa" for the first time.
When your child makes his first soccer goal.
Upon hearing that your daughter has gotten her first menstrual period.
Whenever first-time guests are seated at your Shabbat dinner table.
After you put together the trampoline, just before anyone jumps.
On the morning your child begins kindergarten.
When your child returns to the family Shabbat table after his/her first semester of college. / With the first bite of an autumn apple.

Anita Diamant, How To Be A Jewish Parent

3. When R. Nahman was about to take leave of R. Isaac, he said, "Please, master, bless me." R. Isaac replied, "Let me tell you a parable by which I would respond to your request—the parable of a man who was journeying in the desert. He was hungry, weary, and thirsty, and he lighted upon a tree whose fruits were delicious and its shade pleasant, and a stream of water was flowing beneath it. He ate of its fruits, drank water from the stream, and rested under the tree's shade. When he was about to continue his journey, he said: Tree, O tree, what blessing shall I bestow upon you? If I say to you, 'May your fruits be delicious,' behold, they are delicious. If I say, 'May your shade be pleasant,' behold, it is pleasant. If I say, 'May a stream of water flow beneath you,' Behold, a stream of water does flow beneath you. Therefore I say, 'May it be [God's] will that all the seedlings taken from you be like you.' You, too, [dear Nahman], what blessing shall I bestow upon you?

Knowledge of Torah? Behold, you already possess such knowledge. Eminence? You are already eminent. Honor? You are already honored. Riches? You are already rich. Children? You already have children. Hence I say, 'May it be [God's] will that your offspring be like you.'

The Book of Legends (Sefer Ha-Aggadah), p. 311, #638

RESOURCE SHEETS—"In the Beginning…Having a Jewish Baby"

Session 1-2
Blessings--*Brachot*

בָּרוּךְ אַתָּה, יְיָ אֱלֹהֵינוּ, מֶלֶךְ הָעוֹלָם,

Ba-ruch a-ta A-do-nai, Eh-lo-hei-nu Meh-lech ha-o-lam…

We praise you, Eternal One, Sovereign God of the universe…

RESOURCE SHEETS—"In the Beginning...Having a Jewish Baby"

Session 2
Covenant--*Brit*

2.   And God said to Noah and to his sons with him, "I now establish My covenant
with you and your offspring to come, and with every living thing that is with
you- birds, cattle, and every wild beast as well- all that have come out of the
ark, every living thing on earth. I will maintain My covenant with you: never
again shall all flesh be cut off by the waters of a flood, and never again shall
there be a flood to destroy the earth."

God further said, "This is the sign that I set for the covenant between Me
and you, and every living creature with you, for all ages to come. I have set
My bow in the clouds, and it shall serve as a sign of the covenant between Me
and the earth. When I bring clouds over the earth, and the bow appears in the
clouds, I will remember My covenant between Me and you and every living
creature among all flesh, so that the waters shall never again become a flood
to destroy all flesh. When the bow is in the clouds, I will see it and remember
the everlasting covenant between God and all living creatures, all flesh that is
on earth. That," God said to Noah, "shall be the sign of the covenant that I
have established between Me and all flesh that is on earth."

Genesis 9:8-17

3.   On that day the Lord made a covenant with Abram, saying, "To your offspring
I assign this land, from the river of Egypt to the great river, the river
Euphrates: the Kenites, the Kenizzites, the Kadmonites, the Hittites, the
Perizzites, the Rephaim, the Amorites, the Canaanites, the Girgashites, and the
Jebusites."

Genesis 15.18-21

4.   God further said to Abraham, "As for you, you and your offspring to come
throughout the ages shall keep My covenant. Such shall be the covenant
between Me and you and your offspring to follow which you shall keep: every
male among you shall be circumcised. You shall circumcise the flesh of your
foreskin, and that shall be the sign of the covenant between Me and you. And
throughout the generations, every male among you shall be circumcised at the
age of eight days. As for the home born slave and the one bought from an
outsider who is not of your offspring, they must be c circumcised, home born,
and purchased alike. Thus shall My covenant be marked in your flesh as an
everlasting pact. And if any male who is uncircumcised fails to circumcise the
flesh of his foreskin, that person shall be cut off from his kin; he has broken
My covenant."

And God said to Abraham, "As for your wife Sarai, you shall not call her Sarai, but her name shall be Sarah. I will bless her; indeed, I will give you a son by her. I will bless her so that she shall give rise to nations; rulers of peoples shall issue from her."

…"But My covenant I will maintain with Isaac, whom Sarah shall bear to you at this season next year."

Genesis 17:9-16, 21

5.   The Israelite people shall keep the sabbath, observing the sabbath throughout the ages as a covenant for all time: 17 it shall be a sign for all time between Me and the people of Israel. For in six days the Lord made heaven and earth, and on the seventh day He ceased from work and was refreshed.

When He finished speaking with him on Mount Sinai, he gave Moses the two tablets of the Pact, stone tablets inscribed with the finger of God.

Exodus 31:16-18

6.   "'Now then, if you will obey Me faithfully and keep My covenant, you shall be My treasured possession among all the peoples. Indeed, all the earth is Mine, but you shall be to Me a kingdom of priests and a holy nation.' These are the words that you shall speak to the children of Israel."

Moses came and summoned the elders of the people and put before them all the words that the Lord had commanded him. All the people answered as one, saying, "All that the Lord has spoken we will do.!"

Exodus 19:5-8

7.   You stand this day, all of you, before the Lord your God—your tribal heads, your elders and your officials, all the men of Israel, your children, your wives, even the stranger within your camp, from woodchopper to waterdrawer—to enter into the covenant of the Lord your God, which the Lord your God is concluding with you this day, with its sanctions; to the end the He may establish you this day as His people and be your God, as He promised you and as He swore to your fathers, Abraham, Isaac, and Jacob. I make this covenant, with its sanctions, not with you alone, but both with those who are standing here with us this day before the Lord our God and with those who are not with us here this day.

Deuteronomy 29:9-14

8.   **Elements of a *Brit* ceremony**
        Introductory blessings and prayers
        Covenant prayers and ritual
        Naming and final blessings
        Celebratory Meal- *Seudat Mitzvah*

RESOURCE SHEETS—"In the Beginning…Having a Jewish Baby"

Session 3
Covenant—Brit Chaim

1.   Behold, I am sending My messenger to clear the way before Me, and the Lord whom you seek shall come to His Temple suddenly. As for the angel of the covenant that you desire, he is already coming.

Malachi 3:1

Naming

2.   And the Lord God formed out of the earth all the wild beasts and all the birds of the sky, and brought them to the man to see what he would call them; and whatever the man called each living creature, that would be its name. And the man gave names to all the cattle and to the birds of the sky and to all the wild beasts; but for Adam no fitting helper was found.

Genesis 2:19-20

3.   AND OUT OF THE GROUND THE LORD GOD FORMED EVERY BEAST OF THE FIELD: When the Holy one, blessed be He, came to create Adam, He took counsel with the ministering angels, saying to them, "let us make man." "What will be the nature of this man?" they inquired. "His wisdom will exceed yours," He answered. What did the Lord do? He brought the animals, beasts, and birds before them and asked them, "What should be the name of this?" but they did not know; "of this?" and they did not know. Then He paraded them before Adam, and asked him, "What is the name of this?" "An ox." "And of this?" "A camel." "And of this?" "An ass." "And of this?" "A horse."

 Thus it is written, AND THE MAN GAVE NAMES TO ALL CATTLE, etc. Said He to him, "And what is thy name?" "It is fitting that I be called Adam, because I was created from the ground (adamah)," he replied. "And what is My name?" "It is fitting for Thee to be called Adonai (Lord), since Thou art Lord over all Thy creatures," was the answer. R. Hiyya said: Thus it is written, I am the Lord, that is My name (Isa. XLII, 8), which means, that is My name by which Adam called Me.

Midrash Rabbah, Genesis, XVII, 4

4.   I am the Lord, that is My name; I will not yield My glory to another, nor My renown to idols.

Isaiah 42.8

5.   Moses said to God, "When I come to the Israelites and say to them, 'The God of your fathers has sent me to you,' and they ask me, 'What is His name?' what shall I say to them?" And God said to Moses, "Ehyeh-Asher-Ehyeh." He continued, "Thus shall you say to the Israelites, 'Ehyeh sent me to you.'" And God said further to Moses, "Thus shall you speak to the Israelites: The Lord, the God of your fathers, the God of Abraham, the God of Isaac, the God of Jacob, has sent me to you: This shall be My name forever, this My appellation for all eternity.

Exodus 3:13-15

6.   That same night he arose, and taking his two wives, his two maidservants, and his eleven children, he crossed the ford of the Jabbok. After taking them across the stream, he sent across all his possessions, Jacob was left alone. And a man wrestled with him until the break of dawn. When he saw that he had not prevailed against him, he wrenched Jacob's hip at its socket, so that the socket of his hip was strained as he wrestled with him. Then he said, "Let me go, for dawn is breaking." But he answered, "I will not let you go, unless you bless me." Said the other, ""What is your name?" He replied, "Jacob." Said he, "Your name shall no longer be Jacob, but Israel, for you have striven with beings divine and human, and have prevailed." Jacob asked, "Pray tell me your name." But he said, "You must not ask my name!" And he took leave of him there. So Jacob named the place Peniel, meaning, "I have seen a divine being face to face, yet my life has been preserved."

Genesis 32:23-31

7.   And God said to Abraham, "As for your wife Sarai, you shall not call her Sarai, but her name shall be Sarah.

Genesis 17: 15

8.   When the people of Israel stood at Mount Sinai ready to receive the Torah, God said to them, "Bring me good securities to guarantee that you will keep it, and then I will give the Torah to you." They said, "Our ancestors will be our securities." Said God to them, "I have faults to find with your ancestors ...But bring Me good securities and I will give it to you." They said, "God of the Universe, our prophets will be out securities." God replied, "I have faults to find with your prophets...Still, bring Me good securities and I will give the Torah to you." They said to God, "Our children will be our securities." And God replied, "Indeed these are good securities. For their sake I will give you the Torah."

    Hence it is written: "Out of the mouth of babes and sucklings You have founded strength."

Song of Songs Rabbah 1:4

SAMPLE AD COPY—"In the Beginning...Having a Jewish Baby"

EXPECTING A JEWISH BABY?

3 STEPS JUST FOR YOU

* **LEARN** about birth ceremonies for boys and girls!

* **MEET** other expectant parents.

* **BEGIN** your family's journey to Jewish self-discovery.

3 SESSIONS - $36 PER FAMILY
Wednesday evenings at 7:30 p.m. beginning May 2
At Congregation B'nai Israel, 2710 Park Avenue, Bridgeport

TO REGISTER for "In the Beginning...Having a Jewish Baby" call Gail at **203.335.5058**

In The Beginning

FOR JEWISH AND INTERFAITH PARENTS-TO-BE

Sponsored by the UAHC-CCAR Commission on Reform Jewish Outreach

Congregation offers training for new parents

9593

The early childhood center of Congregation B'nai Israel in Bridgeport, in conjunction with the Union of American Hebrew Congregations, will offer a three-session workshop for expectant parents.

The May programs are open to unaffiliated families and those affiliated with the congregation or the pre-school programs of B'nai Israel.

The workshop, titled "In the Beginning — Having a Jewish Baby" will discuss topics relevant to the spiritual and religious aspects of becoming parents. Topics of discussion will include the blessing upon a child at birth Parents will have an opportunity to write a blessing to be recited at the time of their child's birth. The sessions also will cover the traditions and ceremonies for naming a Jewish child.

The goal of the workshop is to answer questions and concerns expectant families may have about Jewish traditions related to newborns before the actual birth of their child.

Sessions will be led by either Rabbi James Prosnit or by a layperson with expertise relevant to the topic. One of the speakers will be a mohel, the person who performs the Jewish ritual of circumcision for a baby boy.

The three sessions will be held May 2, 9 and 16, 7:30 to 9 p.m. at Congregation B'Nai Israel, 2710 Park Ave., Bridgeport, on the Fairfield border.

There is a $36 fee to cover materials.

Reservations are required. Call Gail Weinstein, Early Childhood Center director, at 335-5058 for reservations or more information.

26

RAISING
A JEWISH BABY?

3 STEPS JUST FOR YOU

- ✦ **LEARN** to bring Jewish spirituality and values into your child's life. Bedtime rituals, too!
- ✦ **MEET** other parents like you.
- ✦ **BEGIN** your child's journey into Jewish self-discovery.

3 SESSIONS - $50 PER FAMILY
Sundays March 11, 18, 25—2001 • 10:30 a.m. to 12 p.m.
At Temple Israel, Boston. Babysitting available

TO REGISTER for "In the Beginning...
And Baby Makes 3," call Ava Harder at the UAHC at
781.449.0404 or **888.291.8242**

In ꤨꤩꤪ
The Beginning
| FOR NEW
| AND EXPECTANT
| INTERFAITH
| COUPLES

Sponsored by the UAHC-CCAR Commission on Reform Jewish Outreach.
Supported in part through the generosity of Combined Jewish Philanthropies

27

Shofar

Temple Beth-El
67 Route 206 S.
Hillsborough, NJ 08844
(908) 722-0674

A member of the Union of American Hebrew Congregations (UAHC)
BethElSom@aol.com
Web Site: http://uahc.org/nj/bethel

Scholar-in-Residence:
January 5 - 7
See page 6

It's Never Too Early to Begin

Rabbi Arnold S. Gluck

We have long aspired to extend the boundaries of our offerings to our members to reach from cradle to grave. In recent years we have made great strides in this regard, creating programming for our older members, and building and greatly expanding Jewish-content offerings in our Early Childhood Learning Center. We have also seen wonderful opportunities provided by our Family Programming Committee, like Parents and Me, a trip to the Jewish Museum in New York, and more. (By the way, it may not be too late to join us for our first ever Family Retreat at Kutz Camp on January 12-14.) Now we are poised to go even further. No, we are not contemplating addressing our members' needs in the afterlife. But we are about to set our sights on the unborn!

Our congregation has been selected by the Reform Movement's Outreach Commission to be a pilot site for a new program aimed at expectant parents. "New Beginnings," a 3-week class designed to help new parents welcome a Jewish baby, will be offered at Beth-El on March 20, 27, and April 3. I will be teaching the class, along with Eileen Kaplan. We will cover a variety of **topics**, **including** the blessings of parenthood, naming and covenanting rituals, creating a Jewish home and family, and raising a proud, well-integrated Jewish child. The program is intended for all people, including interfaith couples, who wish to raise a Jewish child.

We are extremely gratified that the Reform Movement has expressed confidence in our congregation, once again entrusting us with a new programmatic initiative. As many of you know, Beth-El was one of the pilot sites for the wonderfully successful Taste of Judaism program, of which I was one of the authors. To date, that program has reached tens of thousands of people all across the country, and continues to be replicated in a wide variety of venues.

If you are expectant parents, we welcome you to join us for New Beginnings. If you know people who are preparing to welcome a Jewish baby, please let them know about this opportunity.

B'shalom,
Rabbi Arnold S. Gluck

Early Childhood Education Center

From the Director

It was the most unbelievable feeling last week when parents were lined up outside waiting to enroll their children for school in 2001-2002. I was amazed to see that so many parents had heard about our program and just wanted to make sure that their children didn't get closed out. I was so proud to hear them saying that wherever they go someone is talking about the wonderful Jewish content curriculum at Temple Beth-El.

As I was doing the tours of the school last week, I was trying to look through the eyes of a first-time parent looking at a pre-school. *What would I want for my child? What questions would I ask the director? What would I want a facility to look like?* Most parents that come are looking for a clean, safe, bright environment in which their children could thrive. They are interested in the education levels of the staff. *Are they Early Childhood certified?* Our teachers are all

> **We would like to take this time to remind temple families that there are very few spaces left in our school for the 2001-2002 school year.**

certified, and so are our assistants. Many parents ask about the discipline policy. They are happy to hear that we work on positive reinforcement instead of time-outs or making the child feel bad about himself. Many parents ask about our Jewish content program. *What exactly does that entail?* They are thrilled that their children will be learning the daily blessings, the Hebrew color words, Israeli birthday celebrations, Shabbat, tzedakah and much more. Many of them are excited about learning the Jewish content along with their children. They are excited about learning about our temple and possibly joining the congregation, if they aren't members already. The parents are asking questions about how much academics our program

includes. We are pleased to tell them that we pride ourselves on being a school, and not a daycare center. Therefore we expect our teachers to have a daily lesson plan and a theme. Our children are exposed to as much academic stimuli as possible. We believe that the more you teach children, the more they will absorb and learn.

As the many parents signed up and left our school this week, we heard so many of them say, "What a bright, cheery, friendly place for children." We are excited to know that we are fulfilling the needs for so many families.

We would like to take this time to remind temple families that there are very few spaces left in our school for the 2001-2002 school year. If you are interested in seeing our program, please do so as soon as possible, as classes are closing out daily. We wouldn't want any of our Temple Beth-El family closed out of our Early Childhood Education Center.

Eileen Kaplan

Expecting a Jewish Baby?

"IN THE BEGINNING"

... Learn about birth ceremonies for boys and girls...

... Meet other expectant parents...

... Begin your family's journey to Jewish self-discovery.

Tuesday, March 20 and 27, and April 3, 7:30 p.m. $36 per family.

To register, contact Eileen Kaplan, 908-704-1712.

SAMPLE PRESS RELEASE—"In the Beginning...Having a Jewish Baby"

- New "In the Beginning" Program for Jewish and Interfaith Parents-to-be.

Expectant parents, especially first timers, often wonder about how to give their new baby the best start possible. The crib's in place, the childbirth classes are checked off, sweaters and blankets are ready. Now, what about sanctifying the moment and welcoming the newborn into a loving community?

"In the Beginning: Having a Jewish Baby" answers this question.

Through the lens of Jewish tradition couples will explore how religion in general and Judaism in particular can add depth, stability, and wonder to family life. Together with others sharing this exciting time of life and led by an experienced rabbi and early childhood specialist, participants will find out what Judaism says about choosing a name, birth ceremonies for boys and girls, blessings for seeing your baby for the first time and bedtime rituals. No prior knowledge is required.

"In the Beginning: Having a Jewish Baby" will meet on Wednesday evenings, May 2, 9, and 16, at 7:30 at B'nai Israel in Bridgeport. Registration per family is $36.00. Please contact Gail Weinstein at B'nai Israel (203-335-5058) for further information and registration.

B'nai Israel is a specially designated pilot site for this new initiative and was chosen by the Reform movement for its commitment to Outreach and its strong children's, interfaith, and continuing education programming.

"In the Beginning: Having a Jewish Baby" is sponsored by the UAHC-CCAR Commission on Reform Jewish Outreach and will be released nationwide next year. The Union of American Hebrew Congregations (UAHC) is the umbrella organization for 900 Reform congregations across North America.

Session Workshop for Jewish, Interfaith Parents

The early childhood center of Congregation B'nai Israel in conjunction with the Union of American Hebrew Congregations is offering a three-session workshop for expectant parents.

The workshop "In the Beginning — Having a Jewish Baby" will discuss topics relevant to the spiritual and religious aspects of becoming parents.

Topics of discussion will include the blessing upon a child at birth and the traditions and cere- monies for naming a Jewish child. Parents will have an opportunity to write a blessing to be recited at the time of their child's birth.

The goal of the workshop is to answer questions and concerns expectant families may have regarding the Jewish traditions related to newborns before the actual birth of their child.

Sessions will be led either by Rabbi James Prosnit or by a layperson with expertise relevant to the topic. One of the speakers will be a mohel, the person who performs the Jewish ritual of circumcision for a baby boy.

The three sessions will be held at Congregation B'nai Israel on May 2, 9 and 16, from 7:30 to 9 p.m. The synagogue is located at 2710 Park Avenue, Bridgeport.

There is a $36 fee to cover materials and reservations are required. Call Gail Weinstein, Early Childhood Center director, at 335-5058 for reservations or for information.

SAMPLE INTAKE FORM

IN THE BEGINNING...HAVING A JEWISH BABY
Temple Beth El, Somerville

Intake Form

NAME(S): _____
(list caller first)

ADDRESS: _____

_____
City   Zip

PHONE (DAY): _____ (EVENING):_____

E-MAIL: _____

HOW DID YOU HEAR ABOUT THE CLASS? _____

REASONS FOR TAKING COURSE? (Interviewer's notes☺)

Does the caller voice strong feelings? _____

Summary (check all applicable reasons for interest):
Jewish without much background   _____
Jewish wanting more   _____
Intermarried   _____
Deciding how to raise children   _____
Wanting to deepen Jewish experience_____
Considering conversion   _____
Special considerations   _____
Sample Welcome Letter

Sample Welcome Letter

In ▨/▢▨
The Beginning

Dear Friends:

Mazal tov! Congratulations on the new baby you're expecting! And thank you for your interest in "In the Beginning…Having a Jewish Baby."

The goals of "In the Beginning" are to offer participants an opportunity to meet with other expectant parents and to learn about Jewish ways to welcome new sons and daughters, including ceremonies for boys and girls. No prior knowledge necessary.

Please return the enclosed registration form as soon as possible to guarantee your place in the class. Class space is limited, so returning the registration with your $36 registration fee is a prerequisite for attendance. (Make checks payable to Temple Beth-El.)

Each class will meet for an hour and a half on Tuesdays, beginning on March 20 at 7:30 p.m. Directions are enclosed.

Please call me with any further questions you may have. You can reach me at (908) 722-0674. I look forward to hearing from you.

Sincerely,

Eileen Kaplan
"In the Beginning…" Coordinator

enclosure

SAMPLE REGISTRATION FORM

In the Beginning…Having a Jewish Baby

In אלהים
The Beginning

Thank you for your interest in "In the Beginning…Having a Jewish Baby," a Reform Jewish perspective on Jewish family life. We look forward to seeing you.

The class will be held at Temple Beth-El, 65 US Highway 206, Somerville.

NAME(S) _____ (AGES)_____

HOME ADDRESS _____

      CITY/STATE_____ ZIP_____

HOME PHONE _____ WORK PHONE _____

E-MAIL _____ FAX# _____

HOW DID YOU FIND OUT ABOUT THIS COURSE?

WHAT IS YOUR PURPOSE IN TAKING THIS COURSE?

To register for "In the Beginning…Jewish Parenting Made Simple," please send this form to Eileen Kaplan at Temple Beth-El. Be sure to enclose your registration fee of $36, payable to Temple Beth-El.

Driving instructions are enclosed. If you have any questions, please call Eileen at 908.704-1712.

In אלהים
The Beginning

Sponsored by the UAHC-CCAR Commissions on Reform Jewish Outreach and Synagogue Affiliation.

SAMPLE EVALUATION FORM

IN THE BEGINNING: HAVING A JEWISH BABY

PROGRAM EVALUATION

Class Location_____
Instructor's Name_____

I registered for "In the Beginning: Having a Jewish Baby" because I wanted: *(check all that apply)*

_____ Information about Jewish birth ceremonies
_____ Information about how Judaism can help me raise my child(ren)
_____ More information about Judaism in general
_____ To learn more about my own Jewish roots
_____ To learn more about my partner's Jewish roots
_____ To begin the search for a synagogue community
_____ Information about interfaith relationships and how to raise our baby
_____ To know about further classes and reading resources
_____ To meet other expectant parents

Other reasons:

Did this course meet your expectations? ____Yes   ____No
In what ways did it meet your expectations?

In what ways did it fall short?

What was the most helpful about "In the Beginning: Having a Jewish Baby?"

What was least helpful about "In the Beginning: Having a Jewish Baby?"

What would you like to have seen more of and/or less of?

Have your feelings changed about Jewish Birth Ceremonies, Shabbat rituals, values, relevance to parenting, etc. since taking this course?
If so, how?

What else would you like us to know?

Thank you!

In 🄰🄹🄳🄸
The Beginning

Sponsored by the UAHC-CCAR Commissions on Reform Jewish Outreach and Synagogue Affiliation.

ADDITIONAL INFORMATION

We would be very happy to send you additional information and/or put you directly in touch with a rabbi or a synagogue, but we will need your name and address to do this. NOTE: You may submit this page separately if you wish the rest of the evaluation to remain anonymous.

I'd be interested in other classes or group discussions on the following topics:

I WOULD LIKE....
_____ the Rabbi/teacher to contact us
_____ the temple Welcome person to contact us
_____ more information about:
     ( ) UAHC Introduction to Judaism course
     ( ) local synagogues
     ( ) adult education classes
     ( ) interfaith couples groups
     ( ) conversion to Judaism
     ( ) Jewish family education programs
     ( ) pre-school/nursery school

Is there anything else you would like us to know or any other way we can help you?

NAME: _____
ADDRESS: _____
CITY: _____ STATE _____ ZIP _____
TELEPHONE: (w) _____ (h) _____
E-MAIL _____

In בראשית
The Beginning

Sponsored by the UAHC-CCAR Commissions on Reform Jewish Outreach and Synagogue Affiliation.

Dear Caroline Sarah Kornbrek,

Welcome! We at the Arthur and Betty Roswell Early Childhood Center would like to acknowledge your birth with this school T-shirt. We would like to take this opportunity to tell your Mom and Dad about our school. We offer programs starting at age 2.5 years. We have Mommy and Me programs starting at age 1.

So when you are sitting up and ready to come visit the only full Jewish Content Nursery Program in the area, please stop in and chat (or Gurgle). We love our program and would be proud to show it to you and your parents.

At this time, I'm sure Mom and Dad are a bit sleep deprived, overwhelmed and just plain anxious. But, as the months fly by and they get acquainted with their beautiful bundle of joy, I'm sure we might be able to answer educational questions.

Welcome again and hope to meet you in the near future.

Sincerely,

Eileen Kaplan

IV. CURRICULUM FOR "IN THE BEGINNING...JEWISH PARENTING MADE SIMPLE"

See "A note to teachers" and "Suggested common rubrics for each class session" on page 8. Many texts and activities are provided in the curriculum that follows. Make selections based on your own teaching style and the needs of your class.

<u>Be sure to provide babysitting for this class.</u>

In ▨▨▨
The Beginning

"In the Beginning...Jewish Parenting Made Simple"

Session 1:   Parenting as a sacred journey
              Signposts to God: blessings
Session 2:   Signposts to ethical behavior: *mitzvot*
Session 3:   Signposts to a Jewish future: Shabbat and home

Session 1:   Parenting as a sacred journey
Signposts to God: Blessings

Materials needed:
    Class list with names and addresses
    Laminated copies of Blessing sheets (Hebrew, transliteration and English)
        (See Appendix.)
    Copies of any texts and handouts you plan to study (see below)
    Copy of *Hello, Hello, Are You There God?* by Molly Cone
    Good Morning, Good Night CD
    A *Shema* pillow and/or materials

Prior to class write on board:
If the world will ever be redeemed, it will be through the virtues of children.
                                                    Jewish Folk Saying

1. <u>Welcome and introduction.</u>
   Introduce yourself and explain the Reform Movement's commitment to Outreach and interest in this particular program. Tell why you are excited about teaching this class. Also, explain that there will be a short saying posted every week, just as an entrée to the week's session.
   - Review the goals of the program and today's session:
     - A *beginning*: to explore the value of Judaism for parenting a young child.
     - To acquire some simple Jewish tools and practical, age-appropriate information for families
     - To strengthen the bonds within your family.
     - To create a sense of community within the group.
     - To strengthen your connection with the synagogue and the Jewish community. "We want you to know you are welcome and we are glad you are here."
     - To begin to notice the moments of wonder in our everyday lives and make them more special with a blessing.
   - Invite each participant *briefly* to introduce him/herself and tell about his/her child(ren.) Why are they are taking this class now? What is the most burning question each participant hopes the class will address? (Write on board and keep written copy.) Note that all obviously have the common goal of being good parents.

2. <u>Parenting as a journey.</u> The question is: how can religion in general and Judaism in particular help families achieve the goal of being a good parent?? We are not the first to ask these questions. Introduce "Torah" and define. Torah is a Jew's map" for the journey.
   - Briefly set the context for Jewish beginnings (one family setting out on a fateful trip from a small town called Ur in ancient Babylonia—now Iraq—toward an unknown destination, resulting in the oldest continuous religious civilization on earth) and ask a participant to read *Genesis* 12:1-2.
   - Why are Abraham and Sarah going on this journey? What do you think they want or expect from it? Where are they going? How might they feel about being on such a journey?
   - As *you* begin this Jewish journey, how are you feeling? (Overwhelmed, afraid of "not doing it right?" "mapless?") What do you want from this journey? (Consider possibilities: assurances, a map, signposts, direction, ways to raise a good kid.)

—Take a Break—

3. <u>Signposts: Blessings.</u> Judaism gives us maps and signposts for life's journey, ways to make everyday activities special. Why is it important to do that? What is the relationship between the routine and the sacred? Why do we need everyday rituals at all? Discuss.

39

- Ask participants to list some of their own everyday routines—daily activities done regularly, but perhaps with little thought because of their regularity. (Getting up, eating, bathing, going to bed, etc.)
- Read excerpt from Goleman article (or send home as handout.)
- How do Jews mark daily rituals? Blessings: one of the signposts that enable us to make a bridge to God, take notice of everyday moments and raise them to the level of the sacred.
- SUGGESTED ACTIVITY: Read "The Boy and the Flute" from *Hello, Hello, Are You There God?* by Molly Cone.
- Invite participant to read passage from Talmud about 100 Blessings. Why 100 blessings? Why did Rabbi Meir think it was so important?
- How many times a day do you say, "Wow" either out loud or to yourself? As Jews we have a formula for saying, "Wow" as the beginning of a blessing. Read blessing introduction: *"Baruch Ata Adonai Elohenu Melech Haolam."* (This is the "yea God" part.) Then attach what you are saying "Wow" about. How do you think your everyday routines/rituals would change if your family were doing them with God involved? Blessings are important signposts on our Jewish map.
- Examples of traditional ways to mark the routines of daily life and make them special. (Refer to Blessings sheet, p. 48-49.)

  a. Eating a meal: *Motzi.* Read the blessing. Why do you think it is important to bless food, bread in particular?

  b. Bedtime rituals: Discuss bedtime rituals that are working. What makes them work? Explain that it's traditional for Jews to say the *Shema* last thing at night. Read *Deuteronomy* 6:4. What are some ways to make the *Shema* part of your child's nighttime routine? (Sing softly, choose or make a *Shema* pillow to use regularly, sing version of "Twinkle, twinkle little star".) How do you feel as you connect with being Jewish through this ancient blessing? How might you transfer this feeling to your child? Hand out UAHC pamphlet on Bedtime Rituals. How might these help your child feel about the separation of going to sleep? (Share your own experience where appropriate.)

  c. Morning rituals: Greet your child with the joy of reunion. *Modeh/Modah Ani* is a traditional blessing for the morning. Invite participant to read in English. (Stress that any language is ok, even if you only say the words *Modeh/ah Ani*: I am grateful. How do you think a family moment of blessing would change your mornings? SUGGESTED ACTIVITY: Play the *Good Morning, Good Night* CD from Transcontinental Music.

- Introduce the Jewish blessing for new beginnings: *Shehecheyanu.* Hebrew, transliteration, and English. Read in Hebrew and English. What does this blessing say to you? What does "season" mean to you? When might you want to say this blessing? (Consider possibilities: when eating a strawberry for the first time this year, buying a new house, and hearing your child say your name for the first time.) Why do you think we are saying this blessing now? How do you think this blessing would change how you feel about beginnings in your life?

- Remember these blessings are to be practiced. (You don't have to be perfect. If it seems too much or confusing or you feel uncoordinated with it, keep the handout handy, so you can read it. Use whichever language you find most comfortable. Work toward using Hebrew because it is the Jewish language, but remember that God understands all languages. You don't have to memorize it. Just use it and it will become part of your day.)

- Make note of texts from *Song of Songs* 1:15 and 7:7 and refer to Marcia Falk's translations of these texts as blessings for the beloved. Encourage partners to bless each other this week. "The best way to show your child love is to love his/her other parent."

4. Closing
   - Thank participants for their openness and willingness to take risks on this journey. Teach Debbie Friedman's song, "*Lechi lach*."
   - Introduce "car talk" and ask participants to remember what they talk about on the way home.
   - Express your eagerness to see them again next week and announce the topic, another signpost for the journey: *mitzvot*.

In בֿוֹ
The Beginning

Session 2:   Signposts to ethical behavior: *mitzvot*

Materials needed:

> Extra class list with names and addresses
> Extra laminated Blessing sheets
> Copies of any texts and handouts you plan to study (see below)
> Examples of books relating to *mitzvot* for very young children. (See bibliography.)
> Materials to make *tzedakah* box

Prior to class write on board:

Raise up a child in the way he should go, and when he is old, he will not depart from it.

Proverbs 22:6

1. <u>Welcome back!</u> (Take attendance.)
   - Anything special come up in "car talk"?
   - What blessings did participants try out with their child?
   - Review the *Shehecheyanu*. Note that this *brachah* can be said when friends see each other after a time apart, so it's appropriate for this occasion.
   - Review *Genesis* 12: 1. What are some values you were taught in your native land or your parents' house? What are the standards by which you were to live your life? What of these have you kept in your lives and now want to pass on to your child as you start out? Write all on board. These values that guide your everyday life, what you do and how you behave, are the maps for this week's journey.

2. *Mitzvot.*
   - Read and discuss the following texts (or choose one): *Book of Legends* p. 452, #464, *Exodus* 24:7, *elu devarim* (last sentence only). What is meant by "practice" and "study"? Why do you think study leading to action is considered more important than simply doing the action?
   - What is a *mitzvah*? (Consider possibilities: commandments, good deeds)
   - Read "Essential Judaism" about Heschel. Now, any further ideas on what a *mitzvah* is? Have your thoughts changed? In what ways does God giving us *mitzvot* compare with raising your child?
   - Distinguish between a value and a *mitzvah*. Does each call for action? Does each require that we think it's important?
   - There are, by actual count, 613 *mitzvot* in the Torah, divided into 248 positive ("Thou shalt"s) and 365 negative ("Thou shalt not"s.) Relax! We're only going to look at a few today.

—Take a Break—

   - Divide into small groups, each assigned one or more of the following texts: *Psalms* 34:14-16; Heschel, 2nd paragraph; *Elu devarim*, and *Leviticus* 19 (explain "Holiness Code"). (You may, for example, choose to focus only on Leviticus 19 and assign one verse per group or even have each group focus on just one verse.)

Write the following questions on the board for each group to discuss in relation to its texts:

a. Is this a value we hold? Is it a *mitzvah*? In what ways do we do this now? How can we model this value for our child?

b. What might this value mean for us in terms of our own Jewish practice?

c. How could this value become part of our everyday life and rituals?

- For example:

Lev 19:3   What does "revere" or "honor" mean to you? What are ways you might honor your child, so she/he will learn to honor others?

     19:9-10   What are ways you might teach your child to be kind to people who have less? What are some hands-on projects you could start right now? How would you involve your toddler?

     19:17   How might you reprove your child with all your love? In a way that brought no guilt to either one of you?

     19:29   How might the tone of voice you use when you speak with your child effect how your child feels about her or himself. How might that effect how your child speaks with other people?

     19:32   What are some activities you might do with your child to help her/him learn the value and beauty of the elderly, either grandparents or unrelated elderly people? What are some special activities to do with grandparents?

- Groups come back together for overall discussion of questions.

3.   Tzedakah

- Explain concept of *tzedakah*. (Distinguish between "charity" and "righteous" behavior. Distribute Maimonides' ladder of *tzedakah*. See p. 79.)

     SUGGESTED ACTIVITY: Provide materials and/or demonstrate easy ways to make a *tzedakah* box. Discuss ways to involve small children in giving *tzedakah*.

4.   Closing

- Distribute list of childrens' books, tapes and other appropriate materials to help teach about *mitzvot*. Refer particularly to *The 11th Commandment* by The Children of America for lovely examples of *mitzvot*.
- Remind participants about "car talk."
- Next week's topic will be another signpost for the journey: Jewish time and space—Shabbat. Invite participants to bring Shabbat candlesticks and candles if they have them, and to think about what items in their home signal a Jewish home.
- End with "*Lechi lach*."

In 🎲🎲🎲
The Beginning

Session 3:   Signposts to a Jewish future: Shabbat and home

Preparation: Double check that all the "burning questions" from the first session have been responded to either in class or privately.

Materials needed:

> Extra class list with names and addresses
> Copies of any texts and handouts you plan to study (see below)
> Extra copies of laminated Blessing sheets
> Shabbat candlesticks, candles, matches, *Kiddush* cup, wine, *challah*, *challah* cover
> Materials for making simple *challah* covers or dough for braiding *challot*
> A variety of *Mezuzot* from home or temple gift shop, and a *klaf*
> Evaluation forms
> Lists of community and synagogue resources
> Bibliography and/or gifts (stuffed Torah, board book or tape)

Prior to class write on board:

No person is alone when he/she can cling to a chain of tradition in which he/she is the latest link.

Rabbi Joseph H. Lookstein

1. <u>Welcome back!</u> (Take attendance.)
   - Begin with the *Shehecheyanu.*
   - Anything special come up in "car talk"? What *mitzvot* and/or blessings did participants add and/or note with their child during the past week? Was this the first time and, if so, how did it feel? What difference does it make to *say* a blessing or to *talk about* the fact that you're doing a *mitzvah*?
   - Note that this is the last session for "In the Beginning…Jewish Parenting Made Simple" and, after blessings and *mitzvot*, there's one more set of signposts to study today. (Plan future ways to keep in touch at end of the session.)
   - Review *Lech lecha* text. What is God's part of the bargain in this passage? Now that participants are beginning the journey of parenthood, with what might God bless them? What sign does God give the Jewish people? What signs can parents give their children?

2. *Shabbat*—an eternal sign of creation.
   - Ask participants to read the texts on Shabbat aloud. (Resources #2 – 7.) Why is Shabbat so important to God? To us? Note that it is the only holiday mentioned in the Ten Commandments. The fact that it comes every week with unwavering regularity makes it a reliable signpost. And it comes with multiple signs of its own that include blessings and *mitzvot*! And it appeals to every sense (particularly important for children.)
   - Demonstrate and practice *erev Shabbat* rituals. Review both the traditional blessings and others, such as Marcia Falk's in *The Book of Blessings*. (Use Blessing sheets.)

a. Candles   Read *Exodus* 20:8 and *Deuteronomy* 5:12. Why do we light candles? Why two candles? Could it be one? Could it be more? Practice the blessing.

b. Wine   Why do we drink wine/grape juice on Shabbat? What are some ways you can tailor these rituals to your family? Practice the blessing.

c. *Challah*   What is the symbolism of the bread? Explain the *midrash* for why the bread is covered. Practice the blessing.
   SUGGESTED ACTIVITY: Make *Challah* covers or braid *challah* dough that can then be baked to take home.

d. Blessing the children   Why are sons and daughters blessed by expressing the hope they will be like Joseph's sons or the matriarchs? Practice the blessings. Can you add a blessing for your spouse or for friends gathered around your table?

e. *Havdalah* (If time allows; otherwise teach during a Saturday evening reunion.) Why do we do it? Practice the blessings. Alternatively, plan a class reunion on a Saturday evening and begin with *Havdalah*.

- Discuss: What are some ways you could begin celebrating Shabbat in your home? Remember to Keep It Simple. Start small; don't try to do too much. (Tell a story of one of your first *Shabbatot* on your own.) Suggest starting by lighting candles and saying the blessings in Hebrew, if you can, or in English. How do you think having other families and other kids for Shabbat dinner might make Shabbat more fun for your kids? Who would you be comfortable inviting to your home for Shabbat dinner (family, friends, and/or members of the group?

—Take a Break— (Hand out Evaluation Form and insist that it be returned before participants leave.)

3. Jewish Home
   - Celebration of *Shabbat* centers in the home. Introduce the idea of the *Shabbat* table in a Jewish home as a *mikdash me-at*, a small sanctuary. What are some other things you might look for to tell you that a home is Jewish? (List.)
   - Introduce *mezuzah*. What is it? (Pass around a mezuzah with *klaf*.) What does it symbolize? Where would you expect to see one? Why?
       SUGGESTED ACTIVITY: Distribute directions, along with the blessings, for hanging a *mezuzah*. (See *On the Doorposts of Your House*, p. 141.) List local stores where they may be purchased.
   - Read *Deuteronomy* 6:4-9 and 11:18-21, the verses on the *klaf*. Do recognize any part of this? (The *Shema*) How do the two versions differ?
   - Read texts from *Joel* and *The Book of Legends* following. What is the tone of these excerpts? Why are the writers so adamant?
   - Introduce the *v'ahavta*, included with the *Shema* in every worship service. Why are these words, of all Torah, in the *mezuzah*? ("…on the doorposts of your house and on your gates".)
   - What are the key points of this prayer?

- Read *"V'ahavta—When You Love"* by Rabbi Sheldon Marder.

4. Closing
    - Distribute bibliography and resources for further classes for adults and children, nursery school and synagogue involvement.
    - **Collect evaluation forms** and note how important they will be for parents who take "In the Beginning" in the future.
    - Invite each participant to mention one thing that really struck him/her, that he/she will take home, incorporate into everyday life and teach to his/her child(ren). Express your gratitude to participants for their openness to the journey ahead and for what each has brought to the class. Emphasize the "In the *Beginning*" nature of the class and your hope to continue the relationship.
    - End with *Lechi lach*.

In 🔲🔲🔲
The Beginning

RESOURCES FOR "JEWISH PARENTING MADE SIMPLE"

1. Abramowitz, Yosef I., and Silverman, Susan. *Jewish and Family Life*. Golden Books, 1997.
2. *Bedtime Rituals—Transforming Bedtime into Jewish Time*, UAHC Department of Education, 1999.
3. Bialik, Hayim Nahman, and Ravnitzky, Yehoshua Hana, ed. *The Book of Legends*. Schocken Books, 1992.
4. Cone, Molly. *Hello, Hello, Are You There God?* UAHC Press, 2001.
5. Diamant, Anita with Kushner, Karen. *How to be a Jewish Parent-A Practical Handbook for Family Life*. Schocken Books, 2000.
6. Falk, Marcia. *The Book of Blessings*. Beacon Press, 1996.
7. Fuchs-Kreimer, Nancy. *Parenting as a Spiritual Journey*. Jewish Lights Publishing, 1996.
8. *Gates of Prayer*. Central Conference of American Rabbis, 1975.
9. *Good Morning, Good Night: Jewish Children's Songs for Daytime and Bedtime* CD, Transcontinental Music, 2002.
10. Gribetz, Jessica. *Wise Words, Jewish Thoughts, and Stories Through the Ages*. William Morrow & Co., 1997.
11. Grishaver, Joel Lurie, and Huppin, Beth. *Tzedakah, Gemilut Chasadim, and Ahavah-A Manual for World Repair*. Alternatives in Religious Education, Inc., 1983.
12. Kaye, Terry, Trager, Karen, and Mason, Patrice Goldstein. *Hebrew Through Prayer*. Behrman House, Inc., 1994.
13. *On the Doorposts of Your House*, Central Conference of American Rabbis, 1994.
14. Perelson, Ruth. *An Invitation to Shabbat*. UAHC Press, 1997.

15. Robinson, George. *Essential Judaism—A Complete Guide to Beliefs, Customs, and Rituals*. Pocket Books, 2000.
16. Rosten, Leo. *Treasury of Jewish Quotations*. Bantam Books, 1972.
17. Reuben, Steven Carr. *Raising Jewish Children in a Contemporary World*. Prima Publishing, 1992.
18. Siegel, Richard, Strassfeld, Michael, and Strassfeld, Sharon. *The Jewish Catalog*. JPS, 1973.
19. Syme, Daniel B. *The Jewish Home*. UAHC Press, 1988.
20. *Tanakh, JPS Hebrew-English*, The Jewish Publication Society, 1999.
21. The Children of America. *The 11th Commandment*. Jewish Lights Publishing, 1996.
22. *Working With Interfaith Couples: A Jewish Perspective*. UAHC Press, 1991.

Shehechiyanu

בָּרוּךְ אַתָּה יְיָ, אֱלֹהֵינוּ מֶלֶךְ הָעוֹלָם, שֶׁהֶחֱיָנוּ וְקִיְּמָנוּ וְהִגִּיעָנוּ לַזְּמַן הַזֶּה.

Baruch Ata Adonai, Eloheynu Melech Ha-olam shehechiyanu v'keyamanu v'higianu lazman hazeh.

Blessed are You, Ruler of the Universe, You have kept us alive, and sustained us, and enabled us to reach this moment.

Shema

שְׁמַע יִשְׂרָאֵל, יְיָ אֱלֹהֵינוּ, יְיָ אֶחָד.

Shema Yisrael, Adonai Eloheynu, Adonai Echad.

Hear O Israel, Adonai is our God, Adonai is One.

Modeh/Modah Ani

מוֹדֶה אֲנִי לְפָנֶיךָ, מֶלֶךְ חַי וְקַיָּם, שֶׁהֶחֱזַרְתָּ בִּי נִשְׁמָתִי בְּחֶמְלָה, רַבָּה אֱמוּנָתֶךָ.

Modeh ani lifanecha, melech chai vikayam, shehechezarta bi nish-mati bechemlah; raba emunatecha.

I thank you, everlasting Source of life, for in Your compassion You have given me back my soul; great is Your Faith.

Shabbat and Mealtime

Candlelighting

Ba-ruch a-ta, A-do-nai

E-lo-hei-nu, me-lech ha-o-lam,

a-sher ki-de-sha-nu be-mits-vo-tav,

ve-tsi-va-nu le-had-lik

neir shel Sha-bat.

בָּרוּךְ אַתָּה, יְיָ

אֱלֹהֵינוּ, מֶלֶךְ הָעוֹלָם,

אֲשֶׁר קִדְּשָׁנוּ בְּמִצְוֹתָיו,

וְצִוָּנוּ לְהַדְלִיק

נֵר שֶׁל שַׁבָּת.

We praise You, Adonai our God, Ruler of the universe, who has made us holy with commandments and commanded us to kindle the lights of Shabbat.

Family Blessing

For a girl:

Ye-si-meich E-lo-him

ke-sa-ra, riv-ka, ra-cheil, ve-lei-a.

יְשִׂמֵךְ אֱלֹהִים

כְּשָׂרָה, רִבְקָה, רָחֵל, וְלֵאָה.

May God inspire you to live in the tradition of Sarah and Rebekah, Rachel and Leah, who carried forward the life of our people.

For a boy:

Ye-sim-cha E-lo-him ke-ef-ra-yim

ve-chi-me-na-sheh.

יְשִׂמְךָ אֱלֹהִים כְּאֶפְרַיִם

וְכִמְנַשֶּׁה.

May God inspire you to live in the tradition of Ephraim and Manasseh, who carried forward the life of our people.

After the separate prayers for boys or girls, continue for both:

Ye-va-re-che-cha A-do-nai

ve-yish-me-re-cha.

Ya-eir A-do-nai pa-nav

ei-le-cha vi-chu-ne-ka.

Yi-sa A-do-nai pa-nav ei-le-cha

ve-ya-seim le-cha sha-lom.

יְבָרֶכְךָ יְיָ

וְיִשְׁמְרֶךָ.

יָאֵר יְיָ פָּנָיו

אֵלֶיךָ וִיחֻנֶּךָּ.

יִשָּׂא יְיָ פָּנָיו אֵלֶיךָ

וְיָשֵׂם לְךָ שָׁלוֹם.

May God bless you and guard you. May the light of God shine upon you, and may God be gracious to you. May the presence of God be with you and give you peace.

Kiddush
blessing over the wine

Ba-ruch a-ta, A-do-nai

E-lo-hei-nu, me-lech ha-o-lam,

bo-rei pe-ri ha-ga-fen.

בָּרוּךְ אַתָּה, יְיָ

אֱלֹהֵינוּ, מֶלֶךְ הָעוֹלָם,

בּוֹרֵא פְּרִי הַגָּפֶן.

We praise You, Adonai, our God, Ruler of the universe, Creator of the fruit of the vine.

Motzi
blessing over the bread

Ba-ruch a-ta, A-do-nai

E-lo-hei-nu, me-lech ha-o-lam,

ha-mo-tsi le-chem min ha-a-rets.

בָּרוּךְ אַתָּה, יְיָ

אֱלֹהֵינוּ, מֶלֶךְ הָעוֹלָם,

הַמּוֹצִיא לֶחֶם מִן־הָאָרֶץ.

We praise You, Adonai our God, Ruler of the universe, who brings forth bread from the earth.

49

RESOURCE SHEETS—"In the Beginning…Jewish Parenting Made Simple"

Session 1: Parenting as a sacred journey
Signposts to God: blessings

1. The Lord said to Abram, "Go forth from your native land and from your father's house to the land that I will show you. I will make of you a great nation, / and I will bless you; / I will make your name great, / and you shall be a blessing. / I will bless those who bless you / And curse him that curses you; / And all the families of the earth / Shall bless themselves by you." Abram went forth as the Lord had commanded him, and Lot went with him. Abram was seventy-five years old when he left Haran. Abram took his wife Sarai and his brother's son Lot, and all the wealth that they had amassed, and the persons that they had acquired in Haran; and they set out for the land of Canaan.

    Genesis 12:1-5

2. The question "Who's coming to dinner?" has taken on new meaning for researchers who find that household rituals, like gathering for meals are a hidden source of family strength. Casting an anthropologist's eye on rituals of family life, the researchers find that when families preserve their rituals, their children fare better emotionally, even in the face of disruptive problems. "If you grow up in a family with strong rituals, you're more likely to be resilient as an adult," said Dr. Steven J. Wolin, a psychiatrist at the Family Research Center at George Washington University who is a leader of the research on family rituals. This new understanding has led some therapists to help families establish rituals as a way to heal family tensions.

    At the same time, there is growing evidence that such bedrock rituals as a nightly dinner are giving way as more children are raised in single-parent homes or by mothers and fathers with demanding jobs. As a result, psychologists are urging these families to create alternative rituals to fit their circumstances.

    The family rituals that provide psychological sustenance range from daily routines like reading children a book at bedtime to traditions like going the same place for a vacation every year to celebrations like Thanksgiving and graduations to going to church or synagogue regularly. Some families have offbeat rituals, like an "unbirthday party," celebrated at time of year when no family member has a birthday.

    Part of the power of rituals like dinner time, Dr. Wolin and other researchers say, appears to be in offering children a sense of stability and security, dependable anchors despite chaos in other areas of family life. They also teach children in the most rudimentary way the importance of making a plan and seeing it through, even when other temptations, like a tempting television show, come along.

In a study of 240 college students and 70 of their parents, the more meaningful they felt their family rituals to be, the more positive was the students' sense of themselves, and the better able they were to bear up under stresses of the freshman year. "It's not just whether rituals are kept, but how family members feel about them that determines their effect," said Dr. Barbara Fiese, a psychologist at Syracuse University, who will publish the study later this year in the journal Family Process.

Most families begin to establish their rituals while their children are preschoolers, setting up traditions around holidays. By the time the children are 4 or 5 years old, families are able to stabilize daily rituals like dinner time, bath time, and bedtime.

For children 5 to 7, Dr. Fiese finds, rituals are particularly important as a stabilizing force in life. "Their family's rituals give children a sense of security and how their family works together, which is crucial in their own sense of identity," Dr. Fiese said.

"People are returning to family rituals because the world is losing a sense of what's important, offering instead shallow beliefs and sound-bite values," Dr. Janine Roberts, a family therapist at the University of Massachusetts, said. "Family rituals help people affirm what their beliefs really are."

Daniel Goleman. "Family Rituals May Promote Better Emotional Adjustment," *New York Times*, March 11, 1992 (from *Working with Interfaith Couples,* UAHC Press, 1992.)

3. It was taught: R. Meir used to say, A man is bound to say one hundred blessings daily, as it is written, And now, Israel, what doth the Lord thy God require of thee? On Sabbath and on Festivals R. Hiyya the son of R. Awia endeavoured to make up this number by the use of spices and delicacies.

Talmud Menahoth 43b

The principle that the daily service is derived from the dictum of R. Meir, "A person must recite one hundred benedictions every day," was known in Spain as well.

Ismar Elbogen, *Jewish Liturgy: A Comprehensive History*

4. The *Brachah*- the Basic Building Block of Jewish Prayer
How many times a day do we stop and say, "Wow!" (Yes, we know the 60's are over...) Would you believe that the Rabbis of the Talmud (200 - 500 C. E.) recommended that a Jew find 100 opportunities daily to do just that? Of course, the rabbis were a bit more articulate. Each statement of gratitude was required to begin with a standard formula:
Baruch Atah Adonai Eloheinu Melech ha-Olam...

51

Whenever a Jew experienced something wonderful (food, drink, aroma, a beautiful sight, good news) or had the opportunity to perform a mitzvah (one of the 613 commandments in the Torah), he or she marked the occasion by the recitation of a *brachah* specific to that action. This was "Jewish sensitivity training" at its finest. Why were Jews encouraged to say so many *brachot*? The answer was not to please or appease God (who does not need our blessings), but to change ourselves. Each time we recite a *brachah,* we become more aware of the blessings we have received, and we strengthen our resolve to act as God's partners in extending these blessings to others. We become holy by creating distinctions in time and behavior and by living lives imbued with Jewish values.

And to think you can begin doing this with your child(ren) with just six easy words!

Joel Grishaver, et.al. *Tzedakah, Gemilut Chasadim, and Ahavah— A Manual for World Repair.*

5. Twinkle, twinkle, *kokhavim* (stars), shining in the *shamayim* (heavens). If you say the *Shema* tonight, everything will be all right. Twinkle, twinkle *kokhavim*, shining in the *shamayim*.   (Adapted by Renee Boni)

Twinkle, twinkle, Aliza Rose, I love you from your head to your toes. You're my bright, shining light, in our house everything's all right. Twinkle, twinkle, Aliza Rose, I love you from your head to your toes.

6. When to Say Shehecheyanu
Upon eating your first strawberry of spring.
At the birth of a child.
When your baby says "Mama" for the first time.
When your child makes his first soccer goal.
Upon hearing that your daughter has gotten her first menstrual period.
Whenever first-time guests are seated at your Shabbat dinner table.
After you put together the trampoline, just before anyone jumps.
On the morning your child begins kindergarten.
When your child returns to the family Shabbat table after his first semester of college.
With the first bite of an autumn apple.

Anita Diamant, *How to Be A Jewish Parent*

7. Ah, you are fair, my darling,
Ah, you are fair,
With your dove-like eyes!

And you, my beloved, are handsome,
Beautiful indeed!

Song of Songs 1:15-16

How fair you are, how beautiful!
O Love, with all its rapture!

Song of Songs 7:7

8. "Go forth" *Lechi Lach*

Lechi lach to a land that I will show you
Lech l'-cha to a place you do not know
Le-chi lach on your journey I will bless you
And you shall be a blessing (2x)
You shall be a blessing *lechi lach*

L'-chi lach and I shall make your name great
Lech l'-cha and all shall praise your name
L'-chi lach to the place that I will show you
L'-sim-chat cha-yim (2x) *l'-sim-chat cha-yim l'-chi lach*

Music by Savina Teubal and Debbie Friedman

*   *   *

Lech l'cha to a land that God will show you.
Lech l'cha to a place you do not know.
Lech l'cha, on your journey God will bless you.
> And you shall find a blessing,
> And you shall be a blessing,
Your name will be a blessing, *lech l'cha*.

Lech l'cha, may your journey be a bold one.
Lech l'cha, take adventure by the hand.
Lech l'cha, our love will always guide you.
> Go forth and trust your blessing.
> Your name will be a blessing.
Gabriel Meir, *lech l'cha*.

Adapted by Alicia Magal

In בּראשׁית
The Beginning

*Sponsored by the UAHC-CCAR Commissions on Reform Jewish Outreach and
Synagogue Affiliation.*

RESOURCE SHEETS—"In the Beginning...Jewish Parenting Made Simple"

Session 2
Signposts to ethical behavior: *mitzvot*

1. The Lord said to Abram, "Go forth from your native land and from your father's house to the land that I will show you. I will make of you a great nation, / and I will bless you; / I will make your name great, / and you shall be a blessing./ I will bless those who bless you / And curse him that curses you; / And all the families of the earth / Shall bless themselves by you." Abram went forth as the Lord had commanded him, and Lot went with him. Abram was seventy-five years old when he left Haran. Abram took his wife Sarai and his brother's son Lot, and all the wealth that they had amassed, and the persons that they had acquired in Haran; and they set out for the land of Canaan.

    Genesis 12:1-5

2. R. Tarfon and some elders were reclining in an upper chamber in the house of Nitzah in Lydda when this question was raised before them: Which is greater—study or practice? R. Tarfon spoke up and said: Practice is greater. R. Akiva spoke up and said: Study is greater. [In agreement with him], all spoke up and said: Study is greater, for it leads to practice. *Note:* Since both study and observance were prohibited, the question was for which of the two life should be risked. B. Kid 40b

    The Book of Legends, p. 452, #464

3. Then he took the record of the covenant and read it aloud to the people. And they said, "All that the Lord has spoken we will do and understand!"

    Exodus 24:7

4. These are the obligations without measure, whose reward, too, is without measure;
    To honor father and mother;
    To perform acts of love and kindness;
    To attend the house of study daily;
    To welcome the stranger;
    To visit the sick;
    To rejoice with bride and groom; to console the bereaved; to pray with sincerity; To make peace when there is strife.
    And the study of Torah is equal to them all, because it leads to them all.

    Gates of Prayer, p. 53

5. Abraham Joshua Heschel explains this centrality of the *mitzvot* brilliantly, contrasting their central place in Jewish thought with the much less important role of ceremonies:

> Ceremonies, whether in the form of things or in the form of actions, are required by custom and convention; *mitzvot* are required by Torah. Ceremonies are relevant to man; *mitzvot* are relevant to God. Ceremonies are folkways; *mitzvot* are ways to God. Ceremonies are expressions of the human mind; what they express and their power to express depend on a mental act of man; their significance is gone when man ceases to be responsive to them.
>
> Ceremonies are like the moon, they have no light of their own. *Mitzvot*, on the other hand, are expressions or interpretations of the will of God. While they are meaningful to man, the source of their meaning is not in the understanding of man but in the love of God.
>
> Ceremonies are created for the purpose of signifying; *mitzvot* were given for the purpose of sanctifying. Their function: to refine, ennoble, to sanctify man. They confer holiness upon us, whether or not we know exactly what they signify.
>
> From "Toward and Understanding of *Halacha*," in
> *Moral Grandeur and Spiritual Audacity*

Heschel cuts to the heart of another important question: why observe the *mitzvot*? For him it is an existential question. To act in the right way is "to refine, ennoble, to sanctify" humanity. We "confer holiness" upon ourselves by expressing our love- our trust, given that we may not even know what these acts mean- of God. In that statement Heschel echoes the words of the Rav, who seventeen hundred years earlier said that the purpose of the *mitzvot* was "to refine humanity."

The *mitzvot*, then, should be seen as a symbolic expression of our ongoing relationship with the Creator.

In Jewish thought man's first obligation is to make the world a better place...This is why all people must do good deeds even if it is for misguided or selfish purposes.

At the same time, though, the *mitzvot*, by their very pervasiveness, their focus on the quotidian, are designed to place before us at every point in the day our obligation to "be holy" as God is holy. Thus, our intentions are not to be dismissed completely from a consideration of performing *mitzvot*. But it is a keystone of Jewish belief, as the words of the Israelites at Sinai remind us, that one can only come to understand the *mitzvot* by doing them, by imitating God.

George Robinson, *Essential Judaism: A Complete Guide to Beliefs,
Customs, and Rituals,* (pp. 219-223)

6. Guard your tongue from evil,
   your lips from deceitful speech.
   Shun evil and do good,
   seek amity (integrity) and pursue it.
   The eyes of the Lord are on the righteous,
   His ears attentive to their cry.

Psalms 34:14-16

The Psalmist wrote, "Depart from evil and do good" (Psalms 34:15). *Mitzvot* are the Jewish response to problems. Among the *mitzvot* we are instructed to feed the hungry, welcome the stranger, make peace where there is strife, to be kind to animals, to visit the sick, to honor the elderly, to prevent accidents, not to steal, not to take revenge, not to gossip, not to lie and to do *tzedakah*.

From *Family Shabbat Table Talk*, UAHC website

7. You shall each revere his mother and his father, and keep My sabbaths: I the Lord am your God.

    When you reap the harvest of your land, you shall not reap all the way to the edges of your field, or gather the gleanings of your harvest. You shall not pick your vineyard bare, or gather the fallen fruit of your vineyard; you shall leave them for the poor and the stranger: I the Lord am your God.

    You shall not hate your kinsfolk in your heart. Reprove your kinsman but incur no guilt because of him.

    Do not degrade your daughter and make her a harlot, lest the land fall into harlotry and the land be filled with depravity.

    You shall rise before the aged and show deference to the old; you shall fear your God: I am the Lord.

    Leviticus 19:3, 9-10, 17, 29, 32

8. *Kavod* (honor): There was a secret chamber in the Temple in Jerusalem where caring people would leave money. But the poor, those in need, could come into the same chamber and take money. No one ever knew who gave—or who took.

    Mishnah Shekalim 5:6

In the Beginning

Sponsored by the UAHC-CCAR Commissions on Reform Jewish Outreach and Synagogue Affiliation.

In
The Beginning

RESOURCE SHEETS—"In the Beginning...Jewish Parenting Made Simple"

Session 3
Signposts to a Jewish future: Shabbat and home

1. The Lord said to Abram, "Go forth from your native land and from your father's house to the land that I will show you. I will make of you a great nation, / and I will bless you; / I will make your name great, / and you shall be a blessing./ I will bless those who bless you / And curse him that curses you; / And all the families of the earth / Shall bless themselves by you." Abram went forth as the Lord had commanded him, and Lot went with him. Abram was seventy-five years old when he left Haran. Abram took his wife Sarai and his brother's son Lot, and all the wealth that they had amassed, and the persons that they had acquired in Haran; and they set out for the land of Canaan.

Genesis 12:1-5

2. Speak to the Israelite people and say: Nevertheless, you must keep My sabbaths, for this is a sign between Me and you throughout the ages, that you may know that I the Lord have consecrated you. ... The Israelite people shall keep the sabbath, observing the sabbath throughout the ages as a covenant for all time: it shall be a sign for all time between Me and the people of Israel. For in six days the Lord made heaven and earth, and on the seventh day He ceased from work and was refreshed.

Exodus 31:13, 16-17

3. More than the Jews have kept the Sabbath, has the Sabbath kept the Jews.

Ahad-Ha Am

4. The heaven and the earth were finished, and all their array. On the seventh day God finished the work that He had been doing, and He ceased on the seventh day from all the work that He had done. And God blessed the seventh day and declared it holy, because on it God ceased from all the work of creation that He had done. Such is the story of heaven and earth when they were created.

Genesis 2:1-4

5. Remember the sabbath day and keep it holy. Six days you shall labor and do all your work, but the seventh day is a sabbath of the Lord your God: you shall not do any work—you, your son or daughter, your male or female slave, or your cattle, or the stranger who is within your settlements. For in six days the Lord made heaven and earth and sea, and all that is in them, and He rested on the seventh day; therefore the Lord blessed the sabbath day and hallowed it.

Exodus 20: 8-11

6. You shall each revere his mother and his father, and keep My sabbaths: I the Lord am your God. ... You shall keep My sabbaths and venerate My sanctuary: I am the Lord.

    Leviticus 19: 3, 30

7. "That ye may know that I the Lord sanctify you" (Exod. 31:13). The Holy One said to Moses: Moses, in My treasury I have a precious gift- it is called the Sabbath, and I wish to give it to Israel. Go and make it known to them. (p. 486:1)

    When a man keeps the Sabbath, it is as though he had fulfilled the entire Torah, All of it. (p. 486:7)

    "Remember the Sabbath day" (*Exod.* 20:8). R. Eleazar ben Hananiah said: Remember it continually from the first day of the week. If a good portion happens to come your way, prepare it for use on the Sabbath. (p. 488:25)

    In the school of Elijah it is taught: "Remember the Sabbath day, to hallow it" (Exod. 20:8). With what are you to hallow it? With reading of Scripture, with reciting of Mishnah, with [appropriate] food and drink, with clean garments, and with rest [of body and spirit]. (p. 490:42)

    The Book of Legends

8. Remember the sabbath day and keep it holy.

    Exodus 20:8

9. Observe the sabbath day and keep it holy, as the Lord your God has commanded you.

    Deuteronomy 5:12

10. Hear, O Israel! The Lord is our God, the Lord alone. You shall love the Eternal God with all your heart, with all your soul, with all your might. Take to heart these words, which I command you this day. Impress them upon your children, speak of them in your home and on your way, when you lie down and when you rise up. Bind them as a sign upon your hand; let them be a symbol before your eyes; inscribe them on the doorposts of your house, and on your gates.

    Deuteronomy 6:4-9

11. Therefore impress these My words upon your very heart: bind them as a sign on your hand and let them serve as a symbol on your forehead, and teach them to your children—reciting them when you stay at home and when you are away, when you lie down and when you get up; and inscribe them on the doorposts of your house and on your gates—to the end that you and your children may endure, in the land that the Lord swore to your fathers to assign to them, as long as there is a heaven over the earth.

    Deuteronomy 11:18-21

12. Tell your children about it, And let your children tell theirs, And their children the next generation!

Joel 1:3

13. "And ye shall teach them to your children by speaking of them" (Deut, 11:19). From this verse, the sages inferred that once an infant begins to speak, the father should speak to him in the holy tongue [Hebrew] and teach him Torah. And if he does not speak to him in the holy tongue and does not teach him Torah, it is as though he were burying him.

The Book of Legends, p. 635:232

14.

וְאָהַבְתָּ אֵת יְיָ אֱלֹהֶיךָ בְּכָל־לְבָבְךָ וּבְכָל־נַפְשְׁךָ וּבְכָל־מְאֹדֶךָ.

וְהָיוּ הַדְּבָרִים הָאֵלֶּה, אֲשֶׁר אָנֹכִי מְצַוְּךָ הַיּוֹם, עַל־לְבָבֶךָ.

וְשִׁנַּנְתָּם לְבָנֶיךָ, וְדִבַּרְתָּ בָּם בְּשִׁבְתְּךָ בְּבֵיתֶךָ, וּבְלֶכְתְּךָ בַדֶּרֶךְ, וּבְשָׁכְבְּךָ וּבְקוּמֶךָ.

וּקְשַׁרְתָּם לְאוֹת עַל־יָדֶךָ, וְהָיוּ לְטֹטָפֹת בֵּין עֵינֶיךָ, וּכְתַבְתָּם עַל־מְזֻזוֹת בֵּיתֶךָ, וּבִשְׁעָרֶיךָ.

לְמַעַן תִּזְכְּרוּ וַעֲשִׂיתֶם אֶת־כָּל־מִצְוֹתָי, וִהְיִיתֶם קְדֹשִׁים לֵאלֹהֵיכֶם. אֲנִי יְיָ אֱלֹהֵיכֶם, אֲשֶׁר הוֹצֵאתִי אֶתְכֶם מֵאֶרֶץ מִצְרַיִם לִהְיוֹת לָכֶם לֵאלֹהִים. אֲנִי יְיָ אֱלֹהֵיכֶם.

You shall love the Lord your God with all your mind, with all your strength, with all your being. Set these words, which I command you this day, upon your heart. Teach them faithfully to your children; speak of them in your home and on your way, when you lie down and when you rise up. Bind them as a sign upon your hand; let them be a symbol before your eyes; inscribe them on the doorposts of your house, and on your gates.

Be mindful of all My Mitzvot, and do them: so shall you consecrate yourselves to your God, I, the Lord, am your God who led you out of Egypt to be your God; I, the Lord, am your God.

Gates of Prayer, p. 57

15. "When You Love—*V'ahavta*"
When you love *Adonai Elohecha* body and soul
these things I ask of you will be possible:

To answer your children's questions about Me
and believe your answers yourselves
To connect religion to your everyday
comings and goings...

for example,
when you hug them in bed at night
with tender words—*Sh'ma Yisrael*
or when you think to say *Modeh Ani*
in the rush of getting them up and out
in the morning.
To be alert enough
to open doors for your children
in every waking moment
and when they dream.

And finally, to remember just why
all these things matter:

They matter because I, *Adonai Elohecha*,
brought you and your children out of Egypt
to be God for you.
I am your God.
And when you do these things
I will be your children's God.

Rabbi Sheldon Marder

16. When the people of Israel stood at Mount Sinai ready to receive the Torah, God said
    to them, "Bring me good securities to guarantee that you will keep it, and then I will
    give the Torah to you." They said, "Our ancestors will be our securities." Said God
    to them, "I have faults to find with your ancestors ...But bring Me good securities and
    I will give it to you." They said, "God of the Universe, our prophets will be out
    securities." God replied, "I have faults to find with your prophets...Still, bring Me
    good securities and I will give the Torah to you." They said to God, "Our children
    will be our securities." And God replied, "Indeed these are good securities. For their
    sake I will give you the Torah."

    Hence it is written: "Out of the mouth of babes and sucklings You have founded
    strength."

Song of Songs Rabbah 1:4

In ▨▨▨
The Beginning

Sponsored by the UAHC-CCAR Commissions on Reform Jewish Outreach and
Synagogue Affiliation.

IN THE BEGINNING: JEWISH PARENTING MADE SIMPLE

through

Blessings,

Mitzvot,

&

Shabbat

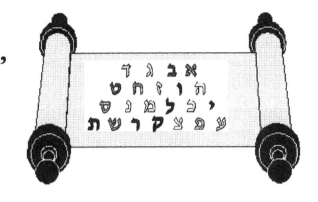

Led by Rabbi Shira H Joseph
Shir Ami 101 Richboro Road, Newtown, PA
215-968-3400

3 Sundays March 11, 18, 25   9 AM -11 AM

Co-sponsored by Shir Ami and the
UAHC-CCAR Commission on Reform Jewish Outreach

Written and Edited by Rabbis Paula R. Goldberg and Shira H. Joseph

IN THE BEGINNING:
JEWISH PARENTING MADE SIMPLE

through

Blessings

Written and Edited by Rabbis Paula R. Goldberg and Shira H. Joseph

Get-Acquainted Jewish Bingo

Directions: Fill in the boxes, listing the values, etc. from top to bottom in order of importance (to you). Introduce yourself to others; have them sign the value which is the number one on their list in the appropriate spot on your card. When you have five signatures in a row (across, up and down or diagonal) you have won Jewish Bingo! (And made some new friends.)

Parenting values	Hopes for children	Favorite Jewish Holiday	Favorite Jewish Object	Most Important Jewish Value

love	healthy	Shabbat	mezuzah	study
limits	friends	Yom Kippur	menorah	charity
honesty	successful	Chanukah	kiddush cup	care of earth
kindness	potential	Purim	seder plate	care animals
safety	kind	Pesach	challah	respect elders
respect	ethical	Rosh Hashana	tzedaka box	honesty
Shabbat	happy	Sukkot	latkes	celebrating
*other	*other	*other	* other	*other

63

Week 1

The Jewish path to finding the WOW! in everyday moments

Objective: Learning and understanding the blessings for food, waking up and going to sleep, and appreciating new things.

Introducing the topic
What is the Root of the Hebrew Word for Blessing?

ב–ר–ך (b-r-ch) -root of "bracha" - from *berech* - knee;
to adore with bended knee.
to fall to one's knees; to bless, praise, congratulate, thank
brecha - swimming pool - in water up to one's knees!
bracha - noun - a blessing; praise of God.

100 Blessings Every Day

Rabbi Meir used to say: A person is bound to say one hundred blessings daily, as it is written , "And now Israel, <u>what</u> does Adonai your God require of you?"

(Talmud Menachot 43b)

Interpretation:
["Ve ahtah yisraeil, **ma** Adonai elohecha shoeil mei itcha." Interpreted as **me-ah, 100**.]

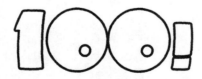

HOW CAN WE GET TO 100?

Would you believe that there are almost 100 blessings that a Jew can say in the regular prayers that are said early in the morning - maybe even before breakfast!!!!

A Jewish prayerbook is called a *siddur* - סִדּוּר, based on the Hebrew word for "order." It is similar to the word *seder* סֵדֶר, the Passover ceremony conducted in a specific order. The prayerbook is composed of a series of blessings in order, our "please and thank you" and praise to God.

Look at the morning prayers found in a traditional siddur:

1 for return of soul
2 entering synagogue
3 for tallit
4 acknowledgment of mercies
5, 6, 7 for tefillin arm, head,
6 washing hands
7 bodily functioning
8, 9 study of Torah
10, 11, 12 priestly blessings
13 for pure soul
14-27 daily miracles
28 for compassion
29 for sovereignty
30 for manifest holiness of Name
31 Kaddish d'rabbanan (scholars)
32 a Psalm of dedication
33 mourner's *kaddish*
34-43 *Baruch she-amar* --for
creation of the world.
44 praise of God
45 for covenant and deliverance
46 for heritage
47 Psalm of thanksgiving
48 Psalm of sovereignty
49-54 Psalms of praise
55 for eternality of God
57 David's praise
58 for redemption (*Shirat Hayam*)

59 praise for power and wonders
60 Readers *kaddish*
61 sovereignty (*Barechu*)
62 for holiness and creation
63 for love and Torah
   (Sh'ma)
64 for redemption
65 For ancestors
66 praise of power
67 for holiness
68-80 Petitionary prayers e.g
wisdom, forgiveness, healing,
etc...
81 for acceptance of prayer
82 thankfulness for daily wonders
83 for peace
84 personal, for acceptance,
humility and peace.
(and this is just for the morning!!)
86-88 Blessings for meals - 3x a
day
89-100 Blessing after meals (4
blessings) 3x a day

WOW! Moments Every Day

Even with the 100 fixed blessings above, we have plenty of opportunity for other kinds of blessings such as: for foods other than full meals; enjoyments such as fragrances and new clothing; experiences of natural phenomena like rainbows; being in presence of beauty or wisdom etc. etc. etc.

Sometimes we can't remember, or haven't learned the specific words for the blessing we want to say. This need not ever stop us from connecting to the holiness in our lives. As some of our teachers have explained, we can learn the first words of the Jewish blessing formula, and then add WOW!!!

"PLEASE" AND "THANK YOU" AS MODELS OF BLESSING

You, as parents, teach your children to say "please" when they are asking for something, and "thank you" when they have received something special.

The Psalmist teaches that all we could ask for, and all we receive, comes from God.

Psalm 24 :1   The earth is the Lord's, and all that fills it

לַיהֹוָה הָאָרֶץ וּמְלוֹאָהּ

When Jews say blessings, it is our way of saying "please" and "thank you" to God, the Source of All.

The Jewish Blessing "Formula"

בָּרוּךְ אַתָּה יְיָ אֱלֹהֵינוּ מֶלֶךְ הָעוֹלָם

Ba-ruch A-tah A-do-nai E-lo-hei-nu me-lech ha-o-lam

<u>Baruch Atah</u> בָּרוּךְ אַתָּה -- Blessed (or praised) are You -- personal, intimate, one-to-one relationship. direct connection and access.

<u>Adonai</u> יְיָ -means, "my Lord, my master -- substitute for Eternal (God's personal name) -- also personal relationship, but recognition of power.

<u>Eloheinu</u> אֱלֹהֵינוּ - our God -- wider circle, includes group, acknowledges covenant with entire people, relationship and obligation.

<u>Melech</u> מֶלֶךְ - king, ruler -- distances the relationship. recognizes power imbalance, more "third person"

<u>Haolam</u> הָעוֹלָם - of the universe -- further distancing while widening the circle of influence to include entire world, sense of majesty.

** Example of a Jewish "Please and Thank You": HaMotzi/Hazan

בָּרוּךְ אַתָּה יְיָ אֱלֹהֵינוּ מֶלֶךְ הָעוֹלָם, הַמּוֹצִיא לֶחֶם מִן הָאָרֶץ.

Ba-ruch A-tah A-do-nai E-lo-hey-nu me-lech ha-o-lam
ha-mo-tzi le-chem min ha-a-retz.

*Praised are You, Eternal, our God, Ruler of the universe,
who brings forth bread from the earth.*

~~
Break
~~

בָּרוּךְ אַתָּה יְיָ הַזָּן אֶת־הַכֹּל.

Ba-ruch A-ta A-do-nai ha-zan et ha-kol.

We praise You Adonai, Source of food for all.

Blessable Moments

What moments, events, things in your everyday life are "blessable?"

_____ _____ _____ _____

_____ _____ _____ _____

Jews regard basic, everyday acts, such as waking up and going to sleep, as blessable moments.

What do we say ?

In the morning:

מוֹדֶה] [מוֹדָה] אֲנִי לְפָנֶיךָ, מֶלֶךְ חַי וְקַיָּם,
שֶׁהֶחֱזַרְתָּ בִּי נִשְׁמָתִי בְּחֶמְלָה רַבָּה אֱמוּנָתֶךָ

[Mo-deh] [Modah] a-ni li-fa-ne-cha me-lech chai ve-ka-yam
she-he-che-zar-ta bi nish-ma-ti be-chem-la ra-bah e-mu-na-te-cha.

I thank You, ever-present Ruler, for re-ensouling me today, with Your love and compassion.

At bedtime:

שְׁמַע יִשְׂרָאֵל, יְיָ אֱלֹהֵינוּ, יְיָ אֶחָד:
Sh'ma Yis-ra-eil A-do-nai e-lo-hei-nu A-do-nai e-chad
Hear, O Israel, Adonai is our God, Adonai is One!

You can help to create holiness in the everyday rituals of family life with your children.

Opportunities for blessing at nighttime:
Create a blessing (see below) for the feeling of a warm bath.
Thank God for our eyes as we read a bedtime story.
Bless our pets for the friendship they give us.
Say the "Sh'ma" to thank God for being God.

Opportunities for blessing in the morning:
Say "Modeh Ani" to thank God for the new day.
Thank God for our teeth as we brush them.
Bless one another with hopes for a good day.

68

Practical Tips:

•Construct a "Sh'ma Pillow"
•Make up your own verse to "Twinkle Twinkle"
   (use your child's name.)

   Twinkle, Twinkle <u>Aliza Rose</u>
   I love you from your head to your toes
   You're my bright shining light
   In our house everything's all right
   Twinkle, Twinkle <u>Aliza Rose</u>
   I love you from your head to your toes

•Read a story about Creation, blessings, etc.
•Make a "please and thank you" blessing album or wall hanging.
•BE CREATIVE!

Other Opportunities To Find Holiness

••For significant occasions in life - birthdays, anniversaries of all sorts, for traveling to new places.

••For first time occasions - first steps, first tooth, first words etc.

••For sensory blessings - for warmth in winter, air-conditioning in summer, for music that soothes us, for soft fabrics, for clean air, fresh snow.

••For people - For teachers, pediatricians, babysitters, grandparents, play-partners and all who keep our lives running as they should...

••For all the "blessable moments" in your life.

Creating Your Own Blessings

Here is a pattern to use to help your children create their own blessings (and help you, too!):

1) **Opening:** Thank You, Blessed are You, We bless You.
2) **Naming God:** God, Eternal One, Adonai, Holy One, our God
3) **Attribute:** Ruler of the Universe, Source of Life, Source of Blessing, Creator of all things,
4) **Event :** "You do x-y-z" (e.g. You open my eyes to new opportunities.)
5) **The "Thank You":** Blessed are You who creates. . .; Thank you...

Example: For your child to thank God for jelly beans.

Thank You   God,   Creator of sweets,   You make jelly beans in all colors.   Thank You for making jelly beans for me to eat!

_____

_____

_____

_____

The Super-Duper All Purpose Truly Jewish Blessing!

בָּרוּךְ אַתָּה יי אֱלֹהֵינוּ מֶלֶךְ הָעוֹלָם
שֶׁהֶחֱיָנוּ וְקִיְמָנוּ וְהִגִּיעָנוּ לַזְמַן הַזֶּה.

Ba-ruch A-tah A-do-nai e-lo-hei-nu me-lech ha-o-lam
she-he-che-ya-nu v'ki-y'ma-nu v'hi-gi-anu laz-man ha-zeh.

We praise You, Eternal our God, for keeping us alive, for sustaining us and for bringing us to this wonderful moment.

✡✡ Blessing Page ✡✡

שְׁמַע יִשְׂרָאֵל, יְיָ אֱלֹהֵינוּ, יְיָ אֶחָד:

Sh'ma Yis-ra-eil A-do-nai e-lo-hei-nu A-do-nai e-chad

Hear, O Israel, Adonai is our God, Adonai is One!

✡✡✡

מוֹדֶה אֲנִי לְפָנֶיךָ, מֶלֶךְ חַי וְקַיָּם,

שֶׁהֶחֱזַרְתָּ בִּי נִשְׁמָתִי בְּחֶמְלָה רַבָּה אֱמוּנָתֶךָ

Mo-deh a-ni li-fa-ne-cha me-lech chai ve-ka-yam
she-he-che-zar-ta bi nish-ma-ti be-chem-la ra-bah e-mu-na-te-cha.

I thank You, ever-present Ruler, for re-ensouling me today,
with Your love and compassion.

✡✡✡

בָּרוּךְ אַתָּה יְיָ אֱלֹהֵינוּ מֶלֶךְ הָעוֹלָם, הַמּוֹצִיא לֶחֶם מִן הָאָרֶץ.

Ba-ruch A-tah A-do-nai E-lo-hey-nu me-lech ha-o-lam
ha-mo-tzi le-chem min ha-a-retz.

Praised are You, Eternal, our God, Ruler of the universe,
who brings forth bread from the earth.

✡✡✡

בָּרוּךְ אַתָּה יְיָ הַזָּן אֶת־הַכֹּל.

Ba-ruch A-ta A-do-nai ha-zan et ha-kol.

We praise You Adonai, Source of food for all.

✡✡✡

בָּרוּךְ אַתָּה יי אֱלֹהֵינוּ מֶלֶךְ הָעוֹלָם

שֶׁהֶחֱיָנוּ וְקִיְּמָנוּ וְהִגִּיעָנוּ לַזְּמַן הַזֶּה.

Ba-ruch A-tah A-do-nai e-lo-hei-nu me-lech ha-o-lam
she-he-che-ya-nu v'ki-y'ma-nu v'hi-gi-anu laz-man ha-zeh.

We praise You, Eternal our God, for keeping us alive, for sustaining
us and for bringing us to this wonderful moment.

71

IN THE BEGINNING:
JEWISH PARENTING MADE SIMPLE

through

Mitzvot

Written and Edited by Rabbis Paula R. Goldberg and Shira H. Joseph

Week 2

The Jewish Path To Holiness Through Action

Objective: Learning and understanding the concept of Mitzvah (sacred obligation) and specifically Tzedaka (righteous giving).

Opening Exercise

Instructions: Imagine that a group of friendly outer space aliens have visited the earth. You, as an ambassador for the "Good Jewish Parenting Association" have been chosen to pack a "suitcase" full of Jewish parenting values for the alien visitor to take back and teach to his/her/its (?) own people. Place 5 values which are most important to you into the suitcase. Pick one value and discuss with another "ambassador" what it means (i.e. how to explain that value to the alien.) Are there other important values that you didn't have room to pack in the suitcase? Place those values in a small pile outside of the suitcase.

Introducing the topic

What is the Root of the Hebrew Word "Mitzvah"?

צ—ו—ה (tz-v-h) -root of *mitzvah* - from *tzavah* -to command;
It has these variations of meaning: order, command, precept, writ, edict, fiat, instruction, mandate, rule, decree, direction, law, bequest
mitzvah/ mitzvot מִצְוֹת מִצְוָה: these are the nouns, singular and plural

This root occurs two times in many blessings:

בְּמִצְוֹתָיו be-mitz-vo-tav   וְצִוָּנוּ ve-tzi-va-nu
sacred obligations (mitzvot)   *and commanded*

Here is the blessing for the mitzvah of affixing a mezuzah to a door.[1] The fulfillment of the obligation of affixing the mezuzah is in putting the words on the door - not in writing them down. The blessing reflects this.

בָּרוּךְ אַתָּה יי אֱלֹהֵינוּ מֶלֶךְ הָעוֹלָם אֲשֶׁר קִדְּשָׁנוּ בְּמִצְוֹתָיו וְצִוָּנוּ
לִקְבֹּעַ מְזוּזָה.

Ba-ruch A-tah A-do-nai e-lo-hei-nu me-lech ha-o-lam a-sher- kid-sha-nu
be-mitz-vo-tav ve-tzi-va-nu lik-bo-a- me-zu-zah.

Blessed are You, Eternal, our God, Guide of the universe Who has made us holy through Your <u>sacred obligations (mitzvot) and commanded</u> us to affix a mezuzah.

 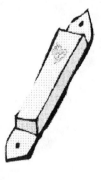

---

1. The mezuzah is placed on the right doorframe as you walk into any room (except a bathroom). It is place about one-third down from the top and tilted with its top inward. Inside the decorative case is a small scroll containing the Sh'ma. The שׁ from the word שׁדי is one of the many names for the Divine.

613 Commandments

The movie *Prince of Egypt* didn't tell the WHOLE story. You know about what is called the "Ten Commandments." In Hebrew these are referred to as עשרת הדברות "aseret hadibrot" -- the **Ten Utterances**. These are the words that boomed forth from Sinai in the powerful first moments of the revelation of Torah. But these utterances are not all the commandments of Judaism. There is much more to the idea of *mitzvot.*

According to tradition, Judaism recognizes many more "sacred obligations" -- six hundred and thirteen!!! How do we arrive at 613? There is a story in the Talmud which explains:

> R. Simlai when preaching said: Six hundred and thirteen precepts were revealed to Moses ... R. Hamnuna asked : What is the text for this? It is, "Moses commanded us Torah, an inheritance of the congregation of Jacob." The word *Torah,* in letter-value, is equal to six hundred and eleven.
>
> $$[\text{ה}=5 \quad \text{ר}=200 \quad \text{ו}=6 \quad \text{ת}=400]$$
>
> To that is added "1 am the Lord your God" and "Thou shalt have no other Gods beside Me" the two which were heard directly from the mouth of the Divine. (Talmud Makkot 24a)

RELAX! We're only going look at a few today.
Of the 613 - guess how many positive and negative.

_____?_____ + _____?_____ = 613!

Rabbi Simlai also explained the categories of the mitzvot:

Three hundred and sixty-five negative precepts,
correspond to the number of solar days [in the year],
and two hundred and forty-eight positive precepts,
correspond to the number of the parts of person's body.

That equals:

$$365$$
$$+248$$
$$\overline{}$$
$$613$$

A positive mitzvah is a sacred obligation which we **should** do. In Hebrew it is called a *mitzvah ta'aseh*. A negative mitzvah, one we **should not** do, is called a mitzvah lo ta'aseh.

Is it surprising that there are more " thou shalt not ..." than there are "thou shalt..." ? Think about one of the first words that every child learns to say. It is the word "NO!" Why do our children learn this word? List some of the "thou shalts " and some of the "thou shalt nots" of your family.

Thou Shalt   Thou Shalt Not

_____   _____

_____   _____

_____   _____

_____   _____

Could you think of more "Thou shalts" or more "Thou shalt nots" ?

The rabbis also gave us another way of dividing the mitzvot. Some, they said, concern actions toward God, such as not using God's name in vain, or even lighting Shabbat candles. These are called *mitzvot bein adam l'makom*. Others concern actions between human beings, such as not stealing or lying, or helping the poor. These are called *mitzvot bein adam l'chaveiro*.

Which category do you have more of on your list?

Holiness Through Action Everyday

The Holiness Code: Leviticus 19

1. The Lord spoke to Moses, saying,
2. Speak to all the congregation of the people of Israel, and say to them,
You shall be holy; for I the Lord your God am holy.
3. You shall revere, every man, his mother, and his father, and keep my sabbaths; I am the Lord your God. . .

9. And when you reap the harvest of your land, you shall not reap to the very corners of your field, nor shall you gather the gleanings of your harvest.

10. And you shall not glean your vineyard, nor shall you gather every grape of your vineyard; you shall leave them for the poor and stranger; I am the Lord your God.

13. You shall not defraud your neighbor, nor rob him; the wages of he who is hired shall not remain with you all night until the morning.
14. You shall not curse the deaf, nor put a stumbling block before the blind, but shall fear your God; I am the Lord...

32. You shall rise up before the hoary head, and honor the face of the old man, and fear your God; I am the Lord.
33. And if a stranger sojourns with you in your land, you shall not wrong him. ..
36. Just balances, just weights, a just ephah, and a just hin, shall you have; I am the Lord your God, which brought you out of the land of Egypt.
37. Therefore shall you observe all my statutes, and all my judgments, and do them; I am the Lord.

The mitzvot come from different places in Torah. Here is the source that reminds us to bless before and after we eat food.

Deuteronomy 8:10

וְאָכַלְתָּ וְשָׂבָעְתָּ וּבֵרַכְתָּ אֶת–יְהֹוָה אֱלֹהֶיךָ עַל–הָאָרֶץ הַטֹּבָה אֲשֶׁר נָתַן–לָךְ:

When you have eaten and are full, then you shall bless the Lord your God for the good land which he has given you.

בָּרוּךְ אַתָּה יְיָ אֱלֹהֵינוּ מֶלֶךְ הָעוֹלָם, הַמּוֹצִיא לֶחֶם מִן הָאָרֶץ.

Ba-ruch A-tah A-do-nai E-lo-hey-nu me-lech ha-o-lam
ha-mo-tzi le-chem min ha-a-retz.

Praised are You, Eternal, our God, Ruler of the universe,
who brings forth bread from the earth.

~~

Break

~~

בָּרוּךְ אַתָּה יְיָ הַזָּן אֶת־הַכֹּל.

Ba-ruch A-ta A-do-nai ha-zan et ha-kol.

We praise You Adonai, Source of food for all.

The Mitzvah of Tzedakah

צ–ד–ק (tz-d-k) root of *tzedaka* from *tzedek* - righteousness

The root has these possible meanings: justice, justness, rightness, correctness, equity, righteousness, fairness.

צדקה, *tzedaka* is the noun which can mean: justice, righteousness, victory, salvation, charity, alms, dole.

Where in the holiness code do we find references to *tzedaka*?

Maimonides "Ladder" of Tzedakah

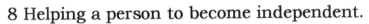

Maimonides lived in the 12th century. He was a great Jewish philosopher and teacher. Maimonides taught us about the Mitzvah of tzedakah - being righteous by helping others. He said there were eight levels of tzedakah. Level one is the lowest and level eight is the highest.

8 Helping a person to become independent.

  7. Neither donor nor receiver know each other.

    6. Donor knows the receiver; receiver does not know the donor

      5. Receiver knows the donor; donor does not know the receiver.

        4. Giving without being asked

          3. Giving only after being asked.

            2. Giving cheerfully, but less than one should

              1. The lowest level is giving grudgingly.

Tzedakah Moments

What moments, events, things in your everyday life are "righteous?"

_____ _____ _____ _____

_____ _____ _____ _____

Opportunities for tzedakah:

Sharing a hannukah gift with one in need; keeping a tzedakah box for coins; make shabbat a time for giving; divide and bring meals for distribution, make a tzedaka box; create you own action plan -- "mitzvah maven"

IN THE BEGINNING: JEWISH PARENTING MADE SIMPLE

through

Shabbat

Written and Edited by Rabbis Paula R. Goldberg and Shira H. Joseph

1

Week 3

The Jewish Path To Holiness Through Shabbat

Objective: Learning and understanding the meaning and value of Shabbat as a family opportunity.

Opening Exercise

Look over the following list of activities and assess whether these activities reflect the Shabbat "spirit" for you and your family. You should be guided by your own personal understanding of what Shabbat, the day of rest, means to you. At the end of this session, you will have an opportunity to reflect once more about these activities and your understanding of Shabbat.

SHABBOS ACTIVITY	Before class		After class	
	Yes	No	Yes	No
going to the shopping mall				
going to the movies __alone __w/ kids __w/friends				
watching CNN headlines				
walking in the park				
walking the dog				
mowing the lawn				
playing a round of golf				
eating dinner out at a restaurant				
driving your child to a friend's birthday party				
doing your income tax return				
telephoning relatives				
going to synagogue				
cooking for a homeless shelter meal				
playing Scrabble™				

שבת שלום

Introducing The Topic

What is the Root of the Hebrew Word Shabbat?

שׁ–בּ–ת (sh-b-t) Saturday, Sabbath, holiday, sitting, ceasing, stopping, to desist, to cease, to strike (work), to observe the Sabbath.

Our English word *Sabbath* is directly derived from the Hebrew word *Shabbat*.

How Do We Know About Shabbat?

ה וַיִּקְרָא אֱלֹהִים לָאוֹר יוֹם וְלַחֹשֶׁךְ קָרָא לָיְלָה וַיְהִי־עֶרֶב וַיְהִי־בֹקֶר יוֹם אֶחָד
ב,א וַיְכֻלּוּ הַשָּׁמַיִם וְהָאָרֶץ וְכָל־צְבָאָם: ב וַיְכַל אֱלֹהִים בַּיּוֹם הַשְּׁבִיעִי מְלַאכְתּוֹ אֲשֶׁר עָשָׂה
וַיִּשְׁבֹּת בַּיּוֹם הַשְּׁבִיעִי מִכָּל־מְלַאכְתּוֹ אֲשֶׁר עָשָׂה: ג וַיְבָרֶךְ אֱלֹהִים אֶת־יוֹם הַשְּׁבִיעִי וַיְקַדֵּשׁ אֹתוֹ
כִּי בוֹ שָׁבַת מִכָּל־מְלַאכְתּוֹ אֲשֶׁר־בָּרָא אֱלֹהִים לַעֲשׂוֹת:

Genesis1:5, 2:1-3
5. And God called the light Day, and the darkness he called Night. And there was evening and there was morning, one day.
1. Thus the heavens and the earth were finished, and all the host of them. 2. And on the seventh day God ended His work which He had made; and He rested on the seventh day from all His work which He had made. 3. And God blessed the seventh day, and sanctified it; because that in it He had rested from all his work which God created and made.

"The meaning of the Sabbath is to celebrate time rather than space."

Abraham Joshua Heschel's, *The Sabbath*

Thoughts:

How do you measure time?

How do you see one moment (day, week, year) as different from another?

What do you think "holy time" is?

כ,ח זָכוֹר אֶת־יוֹם הַשַּׁבָּת לְקַדְּשׁוֹ: ט שֵׁשֶׁת יָמִים תַּעֲבֹד וְעָשִׂיתָ כָּל־מְלַאכְתֶּךָ: י וְיוֹם הַשְּׁבִיעִי
שַׁבָּת לַיהוָֹה אֱלֹהֶיךָ לֹא־תַעֲשֶׂה כָל־מְלָאכָה אַתָּה | וּבִנְךָ וּבִתֶּךָ עַבְדְּךָ וַאֲמָתְךָ וּבְהֶמְתֶּךָ וְגֵרְךָ
אֲשֶׁר בִּשְׁעָרֶיךָ: יא כִּי שֵׁשֶׁת־יָמִים עָשָׂה יְהוָֹה אֶת־הַשָּׁמַיִם וְאֶת־הָאָרֶץ אֶת־הַיָּם
וְאֶת־כָּל־אֲשֶׁר־בָּם וַיָּנַח בַּיּוֹם הַשְּׁבִיעִי עַל־כֵּן בֵּרַךְ יְהוָֹה אֶת־יוֹם הַשַּׁבָּת וַיְקַדְּשֵׁהוּ:

Exodus 20
8. Remember the sabbath day, to keep it holy. 9. Six days shall you labor, and do all your work; 10. But the seventh day is the sabbath of the Lord your God; in it you shall not do any work, you, nor your son, nor your daughter, your manservant, nor your maidservant, nor your cattle, nor your stranger that is within your gates; 11. For in six days the Lord made heaven and earth, the sea, and all that is in them, and rested the seventh day; therefore the Lord blessed the sabbath day, and made it holy.

לא, טז וְשָׁמְרוּ בְנֵי־יִשְׂרָאֵל אֶת־הַשַּׁבָּת לַעֲשׂוֹת אֶת־הַשַּׁבָּת לְדֹרֹתָם בְּרִית עוֹלָם: יז בֵּינִי וּבֵין
בְּנֵי יִשְׂרָאֵל אוֹת הִוא לְעֹלָם כִּי־שֵׁשֶׁת יָמִים עָשָׂה יְהוָה אֶת־הַשָּׁמַיִם וְאֶת־הָאָרֶץ וּבַיּוֹם הַשְּׁבִיעִי
שָׁבַת וַיִּנָּפַשׁ:

Exodus 31

16. The people of Israel shall keep the sabbath, to observe the sabbath throughout their generations, for an everlasting covenant.   17. It is a sign between me and the people of Israel forever; for in six days the Lord made heaven and earth, and on the seventh day he rested, and was refreshed.

The Sabbath is a day for the sake of life. . .Labor is a craft, but perfect rest is an art. It is the result of an accord of body mind and imagination.

Abraham Joshua Heschel's, *The Sabbath*

Thoughts:

How can a day be "holy"?

Why are the other six days also very important?

What is the idea behind including strangers and even animals in the sabba[

ה,יב שָׁמוֹר אֶת־יוֹם הַשַּׁבָּת לְקַדְּשׁוֹ כַּאֲשֶׁר צִוְּךָ יְהוָה אֱלֹהֶיךָ: יג שֵׁשֶׁת יָמִים תַּעֲבֹד וְעָשִׂיתָ
כָּל־מְלַאכְתֶּךָ: יד וְיוֹם הַשְּׁבִיעִי שַׁבָּת לַיהוָה אֱלֹהֶיךָ לֹא־תַעֲשֶׂה כָל־מְלָאכָה אַתָּה | וּבִנְךָ־וּבִתֶּךָ
וְעַבְדְּךָ־וַאֲמָתֶךָ וְשׁוֹרְךָ וַחֲמֹרְךָ וְכָל־בְּהֶמְתֶּךָ וְגֵרְךָ אֲשֶׁר בִּשְׁעָרֶיךָ לְמַעַן יָנוּחַ עַבְדְּךָ וַאֲמָתְךָ
כָּמוֹךָ: טו וְזָכַרְתָּ כִּי עֶבֶד הָיִיתָ בְּאֶרֶץ מִצְרַיִם וַיֹּצִאֲךָ יְהוָה אֱלֹהֶיךָ מִשָּׁם בְּיָד חֲזָקָה וּבִזְרֹעַ נְטוּיָה
עַל־כֵּן צִוְּךָ יְהוָה אֱלֹהֶיךָ לַעֲשׂוֹת אֶת־יוֹם הַשַּׁבָּת:

Deuteronomy 5:12.

12. Keep the sabbath day to sanctify it, as the Lord your God has commanded you. 13. Six days you shall labor, and do all your work; 14. But the seventh day is the sabbath of the Lord your God; in it you shall not do any work, you, nor your son, nor your daughter, nor your manservant, nor your maidservant, nor your ox, nor your ass, nor any of your cattle, nor your stranger who is inside your gates; that your manservant and your maidservant may rest as well as you. 15. And remember that you were a servant in the land of Egypt, and that the Lord your God brought you out from there with a mighty hand and with a stretched out arm; therefore the Lord your God commanded you to keep the sabbath day.

The seventh day is the armistice in the cruel struggle for existence, a truce in all conflicts. . . The seventh day is the exodus from tension.

Abraham Joshua Heschel's, *The Sabbath*

Thoughts:

Are there any ideas, concepts, things etc. that still keep you "in bondage"?

What does "rest" mean to you?

What does "freedom" mean?

Understanding the Shabbat Symbols: Candles

Having just read the two versions of the commandment about Shabbat, do you notice the differences. The two candles that are lit to welcome Shabbat symbolize the two different words which God spoke in the commands.

Understanding the Shabbat Symbols: Kiddush

There are two blessings which are said in the Kiddush; one mentions the sanctity of the day, and the other is the blessing over wine. There is a discussion in the Talmud between two sets of scholars about the proper order of these blessings:

MISHNAH. THESE ARE THE POINTS OF DIFFERENCE BETWEEN BEIT SHAMMAI AND BEIT HILLEL IN RELATION TO A MEAL. BEIT SHAMMAI SAY THAT THE BENEDICTION IS FIRST SAID OVER THE DAY AND THEN OVER THE WINE, WHILE BEIT HILLEL SAY THAT THE BENEDICTION IS FIRST SAID OVER THE WINE AND THEN OVER THE DAY.

GEMARA. Our Rabbis taught: The points of difference between Beit Shammai and Beit Hillel in relation to a meal are as follows: Beit Shammai say that the blessing is first said over the [sanctity of] the day and then over the wine, because it is on account of the day that the wine is used, and [moreover] the day has already become holy before the wine has been brought. Beit Hillel say that a blessing is said over the wine first and then over the day, because the wine provides the occasion for saying a benediction.

Talmud Bavli Brachot 51b

✡✡ Shabbat Blessing Page ✡✡

Candles

בָּרוּךְ אַתָּה יְיָ אֱלֹהֵינוּ מֶלֶךְ הָעוֹלָם, אֲשֶׁר קִדְּשָׁנוּ בְּמִצְוֹתָיו,
וְצִוָּנוּ לְהַדְלִיק נֵר שֶׁל שַׁבָּת.

Ba-ruch A-tah A-do-nai e-lo-hei-nu me-lech ha-o-lam a-sher kid-sha-nu b'mitz-vo-tav
v'tzi-va-nu l'had-lik ner shel sha-bat.

Blessed is the Eternal, our God, Ruler of the universe, who hallows us with
Mitzvot and commands us to kindle the lights of Shabbat.

Kiddush

בָּרוּךְ אַתָּה יְיָ אֱלֹהֵינוּ מֶלֶךְ הָעוֹלָם, בּוֹרֵא פְּרִי הַגָּפֶן.

Ba-ruch A-tah A-do-nai E-lo-hei-nu me-lech ha-o-lam bo-rei pe-ri ha-ga-fen.

בָּרוּךְ אַתָּה יְיָ אֱלֹהֵינוּ מֶלֶךְ הָעוֹלָם, אֲשֶׁר קִדְּשָׁנוּ בְּמִצְוֹתָיו וְרָצָה
בָנוּ, וְשַׁבַּת קָדְשׁוֹ בְּאַהֲבָה וּבְרָצוֹן הִנְחִילָנוּ זִכָּרוֹן לְמַעֲשֵׂה
בְרֵאשִׁית, כִּי הוּא יוֹם תְּחִלָּה לְמִקְרָאֵי קֹדֶשׁ, זֵכֶר לִיצִיאַת
מִצְרָיִם, כִּי בָנוּ בָחַרְתָּ וְאוֹתָנוּ קִדַּשְׁתָּ מִכָּל הָעַמִּים, וְשַׁבַּת קָדְשְׁךָ
בְּאַהֲבָה וּבְרָצוֹן הִנְחַלְתָּנוּ. בָּרוּךְ אַתָּה יְיָ, מְקַדֵּשׁ הַשַּׁבָּת.

Ba-ruch A-tah A-do-nai e-lo-hei-nu me-lech ha-o-lam a-sher kid-sha-nu be-mitz-vo-tav ve-ra-tza
va-nu ve-sha-bat ko-de-sho be-a-ha-va uv-ra-tzon hin-chi-la-nu zi-ka-ron le-ma-a-sei
ve-rei-sheet, ki-hu yom te-chi-la le-mi-kra-ei ko-desh ze-cher le-tzi-at mitz-ra-yim, ki va-nu
va-char-ta ve-o-ta-nu ki-dash-ta mi-kol ha-a-mim ve-sha-bat kod-she-cha be-a-ha-va uv-ra-tzon
hin-chal-ta-nu. Ba-ruch A-tah A-do-nai me-ka-desh ha-sha-bat. Amen.

We praise You, Eternal God, Sovereign of the universe, Creator of the fruit of the vine.

We praise You, Eternal God, Sovereign of the universe: You call us to holiness with the
Mitzvah of Shabbat -- the sign of Your love. a reminder of Your creative work, and of
our liberation from Egyptian bondage: our day of days. On Shabbat especially, we
hearken to Your call to serve You as a holy people.
We praise You, O God, for the holiness of Shabbat.

Challah

בָּרוּךְ אַתָּה יְיָ אֱלֹהֵינוּ מֶלֶךְ הָעוֹלָם, הַמּוֹצִיא לֶחֶם מִן הָאָרֶץ.

Ba-ruch A-tah A-do-nai E-lo-hey-nu me-lech ha-o-lam
ha-mo-tzi le-chem min ha-a-retz.

Praised are You, Eternal, our God, Ruler of the universe,
who brings forth bread from the earth.

✡✡ Havdala Blessing Page ✡✡

(Light the twisted candle)
We give thanks for the Sabbath day that now is ending. We are grateful for its many blessings: for peace and joy, rest for the body, and refreshment for the soul.

(Raise the cup of wine)
The fruit of the vine gladdens the heart, and our eyes open to new blessings.

בָּרוּךְ אַתָּה יְיָ, אֱלֹהֵינוּ מֶלֶךְ הָעוֹלָם, בּוֹרֵא פְּרִי הַגָּפֶן.

Ba-ruch A-ta A-do-nai E-lo-hei-nu me-lech ha-o-lam bo-rei p'ri ha-ga-fen.

Praised are You, Eternal, our God, Ruler of the universe,
Creator of the fruit of the vine
~~~~~

(Shake the spice box and breathe in the scent of the spices)
These spices remind us of Shabbat, now ending. The fragrance helps sustain us through the week ahead until Shabbat returns once again.

בָּרוּךְ אַתָּה יְיָ, אֱלֹהֵינוּ מֶלֶךְ הָעוֹלָם, בּוֹרֵא מִינֵי בְשָׂמִים:

Ba-ruch A-ta A-do-nai E-lo-hei-nu me-lech ha-o-lam bo-rei mi-nei v'sa-mim

Praised are You, Eternal, our God, Ruler of the universe,
Creator of all the spices.
~~~~~

(Hold up lit candle)
The havdala candle's double wick serves to remind us of the separations which enrich our lives -- between evening and morning, holy from ordinary, and Shabbat from the work days of our week.

בָּרוּךְ אַתָּה יְיָ, אֱלֹהֵינוּ מֶלֶךְ הָעוֹלָם, בּוֹרֵא מְאוֹרֵי הָאֵשׁ:

Ba-ruch A-ta A-do-nai E-lo-hei-nu me-lech ha-o-lam bo-rei m'oh-rei ha-eish

Praised are You, Eternal, our God, Ruler of the universe,
Creator of the light of fire.

(In order to better notice the light and dark it is custom to look at ones fingernails in the flickering candle light, to see the separation of the light and dark parts of the nail.)

בָּרוּךְ אַתָּה יְיָ, אֱלֹהֵינוּ מֶלֶךְ הָעוֹלָם, הַמַּבְדִּיל בֵּין קֹדֶשׁ לְחוֹל, בֵּין אוֹר לְחֹשֶׁךְ, בֵּין יוֹם הַשְּׁבִיעִי, לְשֵׁשֶׁת יְמֵי הַמַּעֲשֶׂה: בָּרוּךְ אַתָּה יְיָ, הַמַּבְדִּיל בֵּין קֹדֶשׁ לְחוֹל:

Ba-ruch A-ta A-do-nai e-lo-hei-nu me-lech ha-o-lam ha-mav-dil bein ko-desh l'chol, bein or k'cho-shech, bein yis-ra-eil l'a-mim, bein yom ha-sh'vi-i l'shei-shet y'mei ha-ma-a-seh. Ba-ruch A-ta A-do-nai, ha-mav-dil bein ko-desh l'chol.

Praised are You, Eternal, our God, Ruler of the universe, who separates sacred from profane, light from darkness, the seventh day of rest from the six days of labor. Praised are You , O Eternal, who separates sacred from profane.

(Take a sip of wine. Extinguish the candle in the wine cup.)

~~~~~

The light is gone, and Shabbat with it, but hope illumines the night for us. We look forward to the day when Elijah, the messenger of peace, herald in an era of everlasting peace, when every day is Shabbat.

אֵלִיָּהוּ הַנָּבִיא, אֵלִיָּהוּ הַתִּשְׁבִּי, אֵלִיָּהוּ הַגִּלְעָדִי:
בִּמְהֵרָה בְיָמֵנוּ יָבֹא אֵלֵינוּ עִם מָשִׁיחַ בֶּן דָּוִד:
אֵלִיָּהוּ הַנָּבִיא, אֵלִיָּהוּ הַתִּשְׁבִּי, אֵלִיָּהוּ הַגִּלְעָדִי:

E-li-a-hu ha-na-vi, E-li-a-hu ha-tish-bi,
E-li-a-hu, E-li-a-hu, E-li-a-hu ha-gi-la-di.

Bim-hei-ra ve-ya-mei-nu ya-vo ei-lei-nu
Im ma-shi-ach ben Da-vid, im ma-shi-ach ben Da-vid.

E-li-a-hu ha-na-vi, E-li-a-hu ha-tish-bi,
E-li-a-hu, E-li-a-hu, E-li-a-hu ha-gi-la-di.

Elijah the prophet, Elijah the Tishbite, Elijah the Giladite. May he come to us speedily, and in our days, with the Messiah, descendant of David.

שָׁבוּעַ טוֹב. . .

Sha-vu-a tov, Sha-vu-a tov, Sha-vu-a tov, Sha-vu-a tov
Sha-vu-a tov, Sha-vu-a tov, Sha-vu-a tov, Sha-vu-a tov

A good week a week of peace; may gladness reign and joy increase
A good week a week of peace; may gladness reign and joy increase

SAMPLE AD COPY—"In the Beginning...Jewish Parenting Made Simple"

RAISING A JEWISH BABY?

3 STEPS JUST FOR YOU

* **LEARN** to bring Jewish spirituality and values into your child's life. Bedtime rituals, too!

* **MEET** other parents like you!

* **BEGIN** your child's journey into Jewish self-discovery.

3 SESSIONS – $50 PER FAMILY

Sundays - March, 11, 18, 25 - 2001 • 10:30 a.m. - 12:00 p.m.
At Temple Israel, Boston. Babysitting available

TO REGISTER for "In the Beginning...And Baby Makes 3" call
Ava Harder at the UAHC at **781.449.0404** or **888.291.8242**

FOR NEW
AND EXPECTANT
INTERFAITH
COUPLES

 Sponsored by the UAHC-CCAR Commission on Reform Jewish Outreach.
Supported in part through the generosity of Combined Jewish Philanthropies.

SAMPLE PRESS RELEASE—"In the Beginning...Jewish Parenting Made Simple"

- "Jewish Parenting Made Simple" at Shir Ami

New parents, especially first timers, often wonder about how to give their child the best start possible. Shir Ami, Newtown, will hold a new program entitled, In the Beginning...Jewish Parenting Made Simple" to help answer this question.

Through the lens of Jewish tradition couples will explore how religion in general and Judaism in particular can add depth, stability, and wonder to family life. Together with others sharing this exciting time of life and led by an experienced rabbi and early childhood specialist, participants will find out what Judaism says about how to raise a child to be a "mensch." No prior knowledge necessary.

"In the Beginning: Jewish Parenting Made Simple" will meet on Sunday mornings, March 11, 18, and 25th from 9 to 11 a.m. The cost of this program is $36 per family.

Babysitting will be available.

Contact Beverly Goldberg at 215 968-3400 for further information and registration.

"In the Beginning: Jewish Parenting Made Simple" is sponsored by the UAHC-CCAR Commission on Reform Jewish Outreach. The Union of American Hebrew Congregations (UAHC) is the umbrella organization for 900 Reform congregations across North America.

Temple Beth David to Pilot New Program 9693

The newest initiative of the Reform Jewish Outreach Commission, *In the Beginning*, a program for parents of babies or toddlers, will be piloted for the first time at Temple Beth David, 6100 Hefley St., Westminster.

The Outreach Commission is part of the <u>Union of American Hebrew Congregations</u>' effort to provide programs that serve the needs of Jewish and intermarried families.

In the Beginning will be presented on Sunday afternoons, March 11, 18 and 26 from 3 to 4:30 p.m.

The program will give parents insights and appreciation of blessings, bedtime rituals, Shabbat dinner and other Jewish activities with young children.

Rabbi Michael Mayersohn will lead the sessions. Mayersohn chairs the committee that developed the program.

"We are very excited about serving as one of the first pilot sites for what will become one of the major new initiatives of the Reform movement's outreach program," said Mayersohn. "*In the Beginning* will bring parents together to meet and to learn and explore together what it means to raise Jewish children and create a Jewish home."

The cost for the three sessions is $36.

To register, call 714-894-5448.

Jewish Lifelong Learning

Religious and Hebrew School

Dear Parents,

I hope to see all the parents and children (in your favorite Purim Costume) at the Purim Dinner and Service, March 8 at 6:00 p.m. Rabbi Mayersohn, Cantor Linder, the ECLC director Stella Haynes, and I have a fun Purim Schpiel (Skit) planned for everyone's enjoyment. Surprise and laughter are in store for everyone! You are also invited to join us at the Purim Carnival, Sunday March 11 from 11 a.m.- 1 p.m.. The Purim Carnival is a fun way to spend the day with your family and help support your school. The proceeds from the Purim Carnival will help our Religious and Hebrew School teachers attend professional development opportunities like CAJE. CAJE is the Conference on Alternative in Jewish Education which brings together thousands of Jewish teachers, educators, and rabbis for a week of learning and sharing. See you soon as we celebrate Purim as a community with laughter and fun!

B'Shalom,

Mc.., Lewald-Fass, Director of Lifelong Learning

Religious and Hebrew School
Mark Your Calendar!

March 11	
March 18	
March 23	Fifth...
March 23-25	Sixth an...
March 25	Fifth Grade ,
March 30	Sixth Grade Shabbat Dinner, 6:00 p.m.
April 1	Fourth Grade Family's to Community Mitzvah Fair
April 8-15	NO SCHOOL-Passover br...
	...urim Carnival, 11 ... m.

Have a Jewish Baby or Toddler?
New Pilot Program Starts at TBD

The newest initiative of the Reform Jewish Outreach Commission is a program for parents, Jewish or intermarried, of babies or toddlers. The program, called "In the Beginning," is being piloted for the first time anywhere here at Temple Beth David, at B'nai Tzedek in Fountain Valley and in three other communities across the country. "In the Beginning," on Sunday afternoons, March 11, 18 and 25 at TBD, from 3 to 4:30 p.m., will offer parents insights and appreciation of blessings, bedtime rituals, Shabbat dinner and other Jewish activities with young children. Advertisements have appeared in the major newspapers and the Jewish press to promote the program throughout the community. Temple members, your friends, anyone you know who might be interested, are welcome to participate.

Rabbi Mayersohn will lead the sessions on the Sunday afternoons in March. The rabbi is chairing the committee that has been developing the program with the Outreach Commission over the last fifteen months. The program is for parents and there will be babysitting available. The cost for the three sessions is $36. If you or friends are interested in registering or more information, call 714-894-5448; Stella Haynes, our ECLC Director, is the intake person taking calls and registering people for the class.

We are very excited about serving as one of the first pilot sites for what will become one of the major new initiatives of the Reform movement's Outreach program. "In the Beginning" will bring parents together to meet and to learn and explore together what it means to raise Jewish children and create a Jewish home.

Our Teens are Leaders

a... ~f you may have asked why twelfth grade. TALIT par..., busy... Along attend monthly meetings to discuss current issues and learn how to be a leader among peers.

Students have the opportunity to join an Advanced Camp Leadership track which helps them build leadership skills for camp and retreat settings. Many of the Temple Beth David TALIT teens work as counselors for the fourth-eighth grade BJE Community Shabbatonim.

At these weekends, these teens are not only practicing their newly acquired leadership skills, they are also positive role models for the younger members of TBD. This year 25 teens from Temple Beth David are part of the TALIT program. Keep up the good work!!

In ⬛⬛⬛ The Beginning

Jewish Parenting Made Simple

HAVE A JEWISH INFANT OR TODDLER?

3 EASY STEPS JUST FOR YOU

✦ **LEARN** to bring Jewish spirituality and values into your child's life. Bedtime rituals, too!

✦ **MEET** other parents like you.

✦ **BEGIN** your family's journey to Jewish self-discovery.

3 SESSIONS - $36 PER FAMILY
Beginning Sunday March 11th; 9 to 11 a.m. Babysitting provided.
At Shir Ami Bucks County Jewish Congregation, Newtown

TO REGISTER for "In the Beginning...Jewish
Parenting Made Simple," call Beverly at **215.968.3400**

FOR
JEWISH
AND
INTERFAITH
FAMILIES

 Sponsored by the UAHC-CCAR Commission on Reform Jewish Outreach

92

SAMPLE INTAKE FORM

In ▣▣▣
The Beginning

Today's Date:
Date Materials Mailed:
Interviewer:

Temple Beth David, Westminster
IN THE BEGINNING...JEWISH PARENTING MADE SIMPLE
Intake Form

NAME(S): _____
   (list caller first)

ADDRESS:_____
_____
   City   Zip

PHONE (DAY): _____ (EVENING):_____

E-MAIL

HOW DID YOU HEAR ABOUT THE CLASS? _____

REASONS FOR TAKING COURSE? (Interviewer's notes☺

Does the caller voice strong feelings? _____

Summary (check all applicable reasons for interest):
Jewish without much background   _____
Jewish wanting more   _____
Intermarried   _____
Deciding how to raise children   _____
Wanting to deepen Jewish experience _____
Considering conversion   _____
Special considerations   _____

SAMPLE WELCOME LETTER

In ‫אלב‬
The Beginning

Dear Friends:

Thank you for your interest in "In the Beginning…Jewish Parenting Made Simple."

Our goals are to offer participants an opportunity to meet with other parents of infants and toddlers and to discuss ways to enrich family life through Jewish understanding and practice. Babysitting will be available, so plan to bring your child along as well.

Please return the enclosed registration form as soon as possible to guarantee your place in the class. Class space is limited, so returning the registration with your $36 registration fee is a prerequisite for attendance. (Make checks payable to Congregation B'nai Tzedek.)

Classes will meet from 3 – 5 p.m. on three Sundays, beginning March 10. Directions are enclosed.

Please call me with any further questions you may have. You can reach me at (714) 963-4611. I look forward to hearing from you.

Sincerely,

Roslin Romain
"In the Beginning…" Coordinator

enclosure

SAMPLE REGISTRATION FORM

In the Beginning...Having a Jewish Baby

Thank you for your interest in "In the Beginning...Having a Jewish Baby," a Reform Jewish perspective on Jewish family life. We look forward to seeing you.

The class will be held at Temple Beth-El, 65 US Highway 206, Somerville.

NAME(S) _____ (AGES)_____

HOME ADDRESS _____

       CITY/STATE_____ ZIP_____

HOME PHONE _____ WORK PHONE _____

E-MAIL _____ FAX# _____

HOW DID YOU FIND OUT ABOUT THIS COURSE?

WHAT IS YOUR PURPOSE IN TAKING THIS COURSE?

To register for "In the Beginning...Jewish Parenting Made Simple," please send this form to Eileen Kaplan at Temple Beth-El. Be sure to enclose your registration fee of $36, payable to Temple Beth-El.

Driving instructions are enclosed. If you have any questions, please call Eileen at 908.704-1712.

Sponsored by the UAHC-CCAR Commissions on Reform Jewish Outreach and Synagogue Affiliation.

SAMPLE EVALUATION FORM

In
The Beginning

IN THE BEGINNING: JEWISH PARENTING MADE SIMPLE

PROGRAM EVALUATION

Class Location_____

Instructor's Name_____

I registered for "In the Beginning: Jewish Parenting Made Simple" because I wanted:
(check all that apply)

_____ Information about how Judaism can help me raise my child(ren)
_____ More information about Judaism in general
_____ To learn more about my own Jewish roots
_____ To learn more about my partner's Jewish roots
_____ To begin the search for a synagogue community
_____ Information about interfaith relationships and how to raise our baby
_____ To know about further classes and reading resources
_____ To meet other new parents
Other reasons:

Did this course meet your expectations? _____Yes   _____No
In what ways did it meet your expectations?

In what ways did it fall short?

What was the most helpful about "In the Beginning: Jewish Parenting Made Simple"?

What was least helpful about "In the Beginning: Jewish Parenting Made Simple"?

What would you like to have seen more of and/or less of?

Have your feelings changed about the relevance of Judaism to parenting, Shabbat rituals, values, etc. since taking this course?
If so, how?

What else would you like us to know?

Thank you!

In 🀱🀲🀳
The Beginning

Sponsored by the UAHC-CCAR Commissions on Reform Jewish Outreach and Synagogue Affiliation.

ADDITIONAL INFORMATION

We would be very happy to send you additional information and/or put you directly in touch with a rabbi or a synagogue, but we will need your name and address to do this. NOTE: You may submit this page separately if you wish the rest of the evaluation to remain anonymous.

I'd be interested in other classes or group discussions on the following topics:

I WOULD LIKE....
_____ the Rabbi/teacher to contact us
_____ the temple Welcome person to contact us
_____ more information about:
    ( ) Jewish family education programs
    ( ) pre-school / nursery school
    ( ) UAHC Introduction to Judaism course
    ( ) local synagogues
    ( ) adult education classes
    ( ) interfaith couples groups
    ( ) conversion to Judaism

Is there anything else you would like us to know or any other way we can help you?

NAME: _____
ADDRESS: _____
CITY: _____ STATE _____ ZIP _____
TELEPHONE: (w) _____ (h) _____
E-MAIL _____

In 𝕴𝕹 𝕭
The Beginning

Sponsored by the UAHC-CCAR Commissions on Reform Jewish Outreach and Synagogue Affiliation.

V. APPENDIX
Baby Naming Ceremonies (excerpts)

In ▢▢▢
The Beginning

All the generations, even those yet to be born,
Were present at Mount Sinai and received the Torah there.
Today, we formally welcome our daughter
Into the Covenant of Israel.

Brit Hachayyim
The Covenant of Life

Welcoming
Leora Yaffa Greene
Born November 26, 1999
Erev Shabbat, 17 Kislev 5760
Into the Covenant of Israel

December 19, 1999
10 Tevet 5760

AS WE BRING OUR DAUGHTER INTO THE ROOM, PLEASE READ TOGETHER:

בְּרוּכָה הַבָּאָה תָּחַת כָּנְפֵי הַשְּׁכִינָה

Bruchah haba'ah tachat kanfei ha-Shechinah

May you be blessed beneath the wings of *Shechinah*;
Be blessed with love be blessed with peace.

WE INVITE UNCLE AARON & AUNT JODY TO READ:

Little girl, *B'ruchah Haba'ah*, we welcome you.
You are the latest wonderful chapter in the unfolding of the lives of your mother and father.
You are brand new, a symbol of today and tomorrow;
   your life is a new and clean slate upon which people and events will leave their impression.
You are a bridge over which we who welcome you gaze from this day into future days, from our
   generation in your generation.
You are the newest link in the endless chain of your people's history.
Little girl, *B'ruchah Haba'ah*, we welcome you to life—with love.

DEBORAH AND FRED:
Blessed is she who has come into life. There is a new light in our hearts and our home. These
candles celebrate the birth of our child. Out of the creative darkness, she has come, and these
candles celebrate her emergence into light.

   Fortunate the woman who becomes a mother, for she holds a star.
   Fortunate the man who fathers a child, for he holds eternity in his arms.

These candles celebrate the fire of love out of which this baby was created.

FRED & DEBORAH

Brit Chayyim means Covenant of Life. We see it as an equivalent to a *Brit Milah*, the Covenant
of Circumcision, which Jews perform for their sons. Just as a boy enters into the Covenant
through the symbolism of the ritual circumcision, so a girl enters through the symbolism of
lighting candles and bringing forth light and life.

   Just as the *Ner Tamid*—the Eternal Light of the Sanctuary—reminds us of God's gift of
   Torah, and the Sabbath candles remind us of God's gift of Shabbat, so too these candles
   remind us of God's gift of life.

WE INVITE GRANDMA SANDRA AND GRANDMA BOBBY TO COME FORWARD FOR THE CANDLE LIGHTING

Grandma Bobby: Light was the first of God's creations; as light appeared, it brought with it the possibility of all the wondrous things to follow. We, too, kindle lights—of hope, of understanding, of celebration, of countless new possibilities. This little daughter with whom these parents have been blessed has already brought light into their lives.

Grandma Sandra: May God's radiance continue to shine upon them. May Leora grow to be a source of light to all those around her. May her radiance illuminate the world. May the light of Torah and *mitzvot* be reflected in her shining deeds. And may she help bring the light of redemption to the world. Amen.

LEORA'S GRANDMOTHERS SAID THIS BLESSING JUST A LITTLE MORE THAN ONE YEAR AGO FOR HER SISTER, YAEL. WE INVITE THEM TO ONCE AGAIN RECITE IT FOR LEORA:

ברוך אתה יי אלהינו מלך העולם, אשר בכוחו

אנו מדליקין נר של שמחה וחיים.

Baruch ata Adonai, Eloheinu Melech ha-olam,
asher b'chocho anu madlikin ner shel simcha v'chayyim.

Blessed are You, O God, Creator of the Universe,
by whose power we kindle the lights of happiness and of life.

FRED

Today we perform the act of entering our daughter into the Covenant of the Jewish People. We take on the responsibility of helping her as she grows to observe the *mitzvot*—the sacred obligations of our people—to live by the values of righteousness and justice, and to make this a better world for all.

As she begins her life, she is embarking on a great adventure that will include not only happiness and success, but possibly challenges and sorrow. To live life in today's world will require faith, love, courage and hope.

So God, we pray that You take her by the hand and teach her what she must know to be the best she can be.

Teach her, gently, if You will. She will learn quickly enough that not all people are just, that not all are trustworthy. Teach her that for every scoundrel there is a hero; that for every enemy, there are countless friends.

102

DEBORAH

Teach her the wonder of books, the joy of knowledge. Give her the quiet time of pondering the eternal mysteries of life—the sky, the birds, and the flowers.

Teach her that it is far more honorable to fail than to cheat. Tech her to have faith in her own ideas, even if everyone else says she is foolish. Give her the strength to follow her own conscience.

And finally, bless her with a sense of humor so she may have the strength to withstand each trial of growth she must face.

Bless her, dear God, and give her a wonderful life.

FRED & DEBORAH

Joyfully we bring our daughter into the covenant of our people: a covenant with God, with Torah, and with the people Israel.

Ba-ruch a-ta Adonai,
Eh-lo-hei-nu meh-lech ha-o-lam,
a-sher ki-d'sha-nu b'mitz-vo-tav
v'tzi-va-nu l'hach-ni-sah bi-v'rit
ha-cha-yim.

בָּרוּךְ אַתָּה יי
אֱלֹהֵינוּ מֶלֶךְ הָעוֹלָם,
אֲשֶׁר קִדְּשָׁנוּ בְּמִצְוֹתָיו
וְצִוָּנוּ לְהַכְנִיסָה בִּבְרִית
הַחַיִּים.

We praise You, Eternal God, Sovereign of the universe: You hallow us with Your Mitzvot, and command us to bring our daughters into the Covenant of Life.

DEBORAH

"A Mother's Poem of Thanksgiving"
With all my heart, with all my soul, with all my might
I thank You, God, for the gift of this wonderful child.
I thank You for a healthy pregnancy, a safe delivery and a speedy recovery.

With all my heart, with all my soul, with all my might
I pray for the continued health of this child.
I pray for her to be strong in mind and body,
To grow steadily and sturdily in a home filled with joy.
I pray for her to become a person who greets the world
With passion, courage, humility, humor and patience.

With all my heart, with all my soul, with all my might
I pray for God to watch over me and my family.
I pray for the ability to love and nurture this child
To provide for her and to educate her,
To understand her and to allow her the freedom to grow.

FRED

"A Father's Blessing"
Leora,
May you live to see your world fulfilled,
May your destiny be for worlds still to come,
And may you trust in generations past and yet to be.

May your heart be filled with intuition
and your words be filled with insight.
May songs of praise ever be upon your tongue
and your vision be on a straight path before you.
May your eyes shine with the light of holy words
and your face reflect the brightness of the heavens.
May your lips speak wisdom and righteousness
even as you ever yearn to hear the words
of the Holy Ancient One of Old. (*Brachot* 17a)

Deborah: Many are the mothers, numerous are the daughters who have shaped our people.
Blessed be the mothers, blessed be the daughters.

EVERYONE: May you, Leora, daughter of Israel, be like them:
Patient, as Sarah
Gracious, like Rebecca
Nurturing, as Leah
Loving, like Rachel   (Women of the Torah)

May you be...
Devoted, as Ruth
Dignified, like Naomi
Faithful, as Miriam
Determined, like Tamar   (Women of the Bible)

שְׁמַע יִשְׂרָאֵל

May you, Leora, be...
Wise, like Bruriah*
Compassionate, like Emma Lazarus**
A Lover of Eretz Yisrael, like Golda Meir
Courageous, like Hannah Sennesh°
Hopeful, as Anne Frank   (Post-biblical women)

*Bruriah lived in the second century. She was known as a Talmudic scholar whose views on Jewish law were taken seriously by the rabbis of her own generation. In a time when a woman's voice as not often heard, the Talmud holds her in great esteem.
**Emma Lazarus (1848-1887), a Sephardic Jew and poet, was perhaps the most prominent American Jewish writer of her generation. Her most well known poem is that which is inscribed on the Statue of Liberty.
°Hannah Sennesh, a poet and Jewish heroine, immigrated safely to Palestine during WWII. She later volunteered as a paratrooper to rescue Jews in her native Hungary. At age 23, she lost her life at the hands of her Nazi oppressors.

BIG SISTER YAEL

"On the Birth of a Sister"
Welcome to the world!
You are so small and you cry so much.
People make such a fuss.
I don't know why.

I think I will take care of you
And play with you sometimes,
Because I am big.
I hope you like me.
I hope you learn to say my name.

Sometimes you will pull my hair
But I will not mind,
Unless you pull it very hard.
Sometimes I will fight with you
Because you want my toys.
I hope you will not mind.

Sometimes I will be angry at Mommy and Daddy
Because they spend too much time with you.
I hope you will forgive me.

Thank you, God, for little fingers and tiny toes
Just like mine.
Thank you God, for arms that are large enough to hold one more.

Thank you, God, for a love that is big enough
To include my sister and ME!

זֶה הַיּוֹם עָשָׂה יהוה; נָגִילָה וְנִשְׂמְחָה בוֹ.

This is the day the Eternal God has made; let us rejoice and be glad
in it.

כִּי זֹאת הַבְּרִית אֲשֶׁר אֶכְרֹת אֶת־בֵּית יִשְׂרָאֵל אַחֲרֵי הַיָּמִים הָהֵם,
נְאֻם־יהוה: נָתַתִּי אֶת־תּוֹרָתִי בְּקִרְבָּם, וְעַל־לִבָּם אֶכְתֲּבֶנָּה, וְהָיִיתִי לָהֶם
לֵאלֹהִים, וְהֵמָּה יִהְיוּ־לִי לְעָם.

This is the covenant I will make with the House of Israel in time
to come, says the Eternal One: I will put My Teaching within them,
and engrave it on their hearts; I will be their God, and they shall be
My people.

Explanation of Leora Yaffa's name
לִיאוֹרָה יָפָה בַּת טוֹבִיָּה לֵוִי הַכֹּהֵן חֲבוּרָה לֵאָה
& Reflections on the Torah portion of the week she was born

אֱלֹהֵינוּ וֵאלֹהֵי אֲבוֹתֵינוּ וְאִמּוֹתֵינוּ, קַיֵּם אֶת־הַיַּלְדָּה הַזֹּאת לְאָבִיהָ וּלְאִמָּהּ,
וְיִקָּרֵא שְׁמָהּ בְּיִשְׂרָאֵל . . . . יִשְׂמַח הָאָב בְּיוֹצֵאת חֲלָצָיו
וְתָגֵל אִמָּהּ בִּפְרִי בִטְנָהּ. זֹאת הַקְּטַנָּה גְּדוֹלָה תִּהְיֶה. כְּשֵׁם שֶׁנִּכְנְסָה
לַבְּרִית כֵּן תִּכָּנֵס לַתּוֹרָה, לְחֻפָּה, וּלְמַעֲשִׂים טוֹבִים.

DEBORAH AND FRED

Our God and God of our mothers and fathers, sustain this child, and let her be known in the House of Israel as *Leora Yaffa bat Tuvia Levi Hacohen u'Devorah Leah.* May she bring us much joy. As she has entered into the Covenant of Life, so may she enter into the life of Torah, marriage and family, and the practice of goodness to others.
WE INVITE OUR FAMILY MEMBERS TO SAY TO LEORA YAFFA

May the One who blessed our fathers Abraham, Isaac, and Jacob, and our mothers Sarah, Rebecca, Leah and Rachel, bless this child and keep her from all harm. May her parents help her to dedicate her life in faithfulness to God, her heart receptive to Torah and *mitzvot.* Then shall she bring blessing to her parents, her people, and all the world. Amen.

מִי שֶׁבֵּרַךְ אֲבוֹתֵינוּ אַבְרָהָם, יִצְחָק, וְיַעֲקֹב, וְאִמּוֹתֵינוּ שָׂרָה, רִבְקָה,
לֵאָה, וְרָחֵל, הוּא יְבָרֵךְ אֶת־הַיַּלְדָּה הָרַכָּה וְיִשְׁמְרֶהָ מִכָּל־צָרָה וְצוּקָה.
וִיזַכּוּ הוֹרֶיהָ לְגַדְּלָהּ, לְחַנְּכָהּ וּלְחַכְּמָהּ. וְיִהְיוּ יָדֶיהָ וְלִבָּהּ לְאֵל אֱמוּנָה,
וְנֹאמַר: אָמֵן.

Mi shebeirach avoteinu Avraham, Yitzchak, v'Ya'akov, v'imoteinu Sarah, Rivka, Leah v'Rachel, hu y'varech et-hayaldah harakah v'yishm're-ha mikol-tzarah v'tzukah. V'yizku hor-e-ha l'gadlah, l'chan'chah u'l'chakmah. V'yihiyu yadeha v'libah l'Eil emunah, V'nomar: Amen.

WE INVITE OUR FRIENDS AND FAMILY TO SAY TO DEBORAH AND FRED

Friends, may you dedicate yourselves to give your holiest gifts—love and respect—to your daughter, whom you have brought to be named, and may you ever give freely of yourselves, so that in time's fullness your love will bestow upon this child the gift of freedom. May joy ever accompany such giving and receiving.

PLEASE READ TOGETHER:

Build us a Daughter of Israel, O God, whose heart will be clear, whose goals will be high; one who will learn to love herself, so that she may better love others. A daughter who will learn to laugh, yet never forget how to weep; one who will reach into the future, yet never forget the past.

After all these things are hers, this we pray, enough sense of humor that she will always be serious but never take herself too seriously. Give her humility so that she may always remember the simplicity of true greatness, the open mind of true wisdom, the meekness of true strength; then we, her friends and family, will dare to whisper, "We, too, have been enriched."

107

JUST AS GRANDPA LOWELL RECITED THESE WORDS FOR LEORA'S LITTLE SISTER A LITTLE OVER A
YEAR AGO, WE INVITE HIM ONCE AGAIN TO RECITE THE *KIDDUSH*—THE BLESSING OVER THE WINE

May Leora's life be free and open and fulfilled.
May she learn with enthusiasm.
May she trust with openness.
May she laugh with joy.
And when she cries, may it be with purpose.
May her life's goals be lofty and noble.
And when she falls, may she find pride in getting up to try again.
May she live and love with passion.

Ba-ruch a-ta Adonai,　　　　　　בָּרוּךְ אַתָּה יי

Eh-lo-hei-nu meh-lech ha-o-lam,　　אֱלֹהֵינוּ מֶלֶךְ הָעוֹלָם,

bo-rei p'ri ha-ga-fen.　　　　　　בּוֹרֵא פְּרִי הַגָּפֶן.

We praise You, Eternal God, Sovereign of the universe, Creator of the
fruit of the vine.

OUR FRIEND, STUDENT CANTOR DAVID MUCHNICK

Y'va-reh-ch'cha Adonai v'yish-m'reh-cha.　　יְבָרֶכְךָ יהוה וְיִשְׁמְרֶךָ.

Ya-eir Adonai pa-nav ei-leh-cha　　　　　יָאֵר יהוה פָּנָיו אֵלֶיךָ

vi-chu-neh-ka.　　　　　　　　　　　וִיחֻנֶּךָ.

Yi-sa Adonai pa-nav ei-leh-cha　　　　　יִשָּׂא יהוה פָּנָיו אֵלֶיךָ

v'ya-seim l'cha sha-lom.　　　　　　　וְיָשֵׂם לְךָ שָׁלוֹם.

May God bless you and keep you. May God look kindly upon you,
and be gracious to you. May God reach out to You in tenderness, and
give you peace.

"On the birth of a Grandchild"

Grandpa Lowell:　　　In the Talmud, there is a story of an old man who was seen planting a
　　　　　　　　　　carob tree as the king rode by. "Old Man," the king said, "how many
　　　　　　　　　　years will it be before that tree bears fruit?" The Old Man replied:
　　　　　　　　　　"Perhaps seventy years." The king asked: "Do you really expect to be
　　　　　　　　　　alive to eat the fruit of that tree?" "No," answered the man. "But just as I
　　　　　　　　　　found the world fruitful when I was born, so I plant trees, that later
　　　　　　　　　　generations may eat thereof."

Grandma Bobby:	We are thankful for the blessing You have bestowed upon us in our lives. Now we have been granted a new grandchild to love, the opening of a new page in our families' chronicles. May this child grow up in health and happiness.
Grandma Sandra:	May her dear parents find much joy in the years that lie before them. O God of life, may they raise their child with wisdom and understanding, teaching her the ways of righteousness, leading her to the study of Torah and the practice of love and kindness.
Grandparents:	May we, too, be granted the joy of seeing her develop all her gifts, and the gratification of helping her to fulfill the best that is in her. Then our prayer shall have found its answer: the days and years to come shall be for us times of peace and fulfillment. Amen.

Ba-ruch a-ta Adonai,
E-lo-hei-nu meh-lech ha-o-lam,
sheh-heh-cheh-ya-nu, v'ki-y'ma-nu,
v'hi-gi-a-nu la-z'man ha-zeh.

בָּרוּךְ אַתָּה יי
אֱלֹהֵינוּ מֶלֶךְ הָעוֹלָם,
שֶׁהֶחֱיָנוּ וְקִיְּמָנוּ
וְהִגִּיעָנוּ לַזְּמַן הַזֶּה.

We praise You, Eternal God, Sovereign of the universe, for giving us life, for sustaining us, and for enabling us to reach this season.

IT IS A JEWISH TRADITION TO END A *SIMCHA* SINGING *SIMAN TOV*. PLEASE JOIN WITH US!

Si-man tov u-ma-zal tov
U-ma-zal tov v'-si-man tov
Y'-hei la-nu

Y'-hei la-nu y'-hei la-nu
U-l'-chol Yis-ra-eil

סִימָן טוֹב וּמַזָּל טוֹב
וּמַזָּל טוֹב וְסִימָן טוֹב
יְהֵא לָנוּ

יְהֵא לָנוּ יְהֵא לָנוּ
וּלְכָל־יִשְׂרָאֵל

It is a good and a lucky sign for us and all Israel!

In honor of Leora Yaffa's *Brit*, Deborah and Fred have made contributions to the Make-a-Wish Foundation and the New Israel Fund.

- "Light" is from Debra Cantor and Rebecca Jacobs, "Brit Banot," *Kerem: Creative Explorations in Judaism*, Winter 1992-1993/5753, © 1993 Rabbinical Assembly, pp. 49-50.
- "A Mother's Poem of Thanksgiving" adapted by Rabbi Maggie Wenig from the poem by Rabbi Judith Shanks
- "A Father's Blessing" (*Brachot* 17a) is translated in *V'taher Libbenu* of Congregation Beth El of the Sudbury.
- "On the Birth of a Sister" Is by Sandy Eisenberg Sasso, 1998.
- Prayers from *On the Doorposts of Your House: Prayers and Ceremonies for the Jewish home* (New York: CCAR, 1994).
- "On the birth of a Grandchild" by Chaim Stern in *Doorposts*.
- Additional readings were from Rabbi Joel Goor, William Dreskin, Wendy Spears and Judith Beiner.

Brit Bat
Baby Naming

Natalie Price Harder
Nechama Faige

November 11, 2000

- **Rabbi Sisenwine:** Welcoming Remarks
- **Natalie is brought in by Pop Henry, Grandma Peg and Auntie Roz**
- **Rabbi Sisenwine:**

B'ruchah ha-ba-ah b'sheim Adonai.
May she who enters be blessed in God's name.

B'ruchim ha-ba-im b'sheim Adonai.
May all who join her, to celebrate with her, also be blessed in God's name.

- **Ava and Bruce:** [explain *Huppah* and poles]
Natalie, your father and I stood under this *Huppah* three years ago to be joined together as husband and wife. Beloved friends and family created each of the squares. Just as we all are joining together today for this celebration, a joining together in love, so did your Grandma Peg fashion each square of our *Huppah* together, binding together with love each one to make the whole. We are so proud to be able to surround you with our love and the love of this *Huppah* today.

Natalie, these rough poles that support this beautiful *Huppah* are the same poles that supported it when your mother and I were married. They come from the land I grew up on in Wisconsin. To me they represent the strength and support I feel and I hope you will feel, from my heritage and my family. They also represent the natural rhythm and balance of all created things. We hope you will rejoice and respect the natural wonder that is God.

- **Rabbi Sisenwine:** explains *Shabbat* candles

- **Ava:**
We have been blessed with the gift of new life. With the privilege of parenthood we accept the responsibility of guiding our daughter toward becoming a caring and loving person with a sense of her own worth and a respect for the worth of others. Natalie, your father and I have taken such delight in your beauty and wonder.

- **Bruce**
You have added a new dimension to my life and to the life I share with Ava. You bring happiness and wonder into our lives whenever we hear your new voice or see your eyes. You grab and hold our focus and our hearts whenever you look at us.

You are the continuation and the next step of multiple heritages. We want to help you learn where you come from so you can choose where you are going. Expectedly and like any proud parents, we want to help you live a happy, fulfilled and complete life. What is unexpected is that I think you will help us be the best that we can be. You have made us happier than we imagined possible.

- **Ava and Bruce:**

We give our daughter the gift of tradition: A heritage of strength and scholarship, of love of Torah, love for the Jewish people and love for all of humanity. This child need never wonder who she is or where she belongs. May we always help her remember this.

We also give her the gift of unconditional love. May she always know that her family cherishes her and values her not only for her achievements, but because she is a gift that we are privileged to share. It is with great joy, in the presence of all those dear to us, that we link our daughter with the Jewish people and with all of humanity.

♦ **Rabbi Sisenwine:** [explains Elijah's chair]
In Jewish tradition, Elijah the Prophet represents the coming of the Messianic time. Elijah is present at the covenant whose sign is circumcision, at the Pesach seder, at the weekly *havdalah* ceremony; and is known as the guardian of young children. Elijah's presence at this covenant ceremony bids us look through the life of one child to the fulfillment of all life.

♦ **Rabbi Sisenwine:** [prayer for parents and baby]

♦ **Cindy Siagel:**
The philosopher, Martin Buber, once wrote that every person born into this world represents something new, something original and unique. It is the duty of every person to know that she is unique, to consider that there has never been someone like her in this world. Each new creation is in the image of God, yet every person is an individual, called upon to fulfill her particularity.

♦ **Rabbi Sisenwine:**
It is the tradition of the Jewish people to give expression to a person's uniqueness through the act of naming.

Our God and God of all generations, May You who blessed our ancestors – Abraham and Sarah, Isaac and Rebecca, Jacob, Leah and Rachel – bless this child with life and health. May she be a joy to her parents, bringing honor to all people, blessing to humanity, and glory to the Name of God.

Now, in the presence of loved ones and in the presence of the Holy One, we give this child the name NATALIE PRICE, NECHAMA FAIGE. Let this become a name that is honored and respected for wisdom and good deeds. May God's blessing rest upon this name now and always.

♦ **Ava:** [Introduces the name "Natalie"]
Natalie has been given her first name in memory of my maternal grandmother, Natalie, my Nana, who we lost almost 3 years ago, a few months after Bruce and I were married. My Nana was a teacher...a first grade teacher. She loved to teach. My Nana also loved to learn. She got her Masters Degree, which was way outside the norm for her generation. I remember my Nana as loving Judaism, loving to read, loving her friends and family. Natalie, it's fitting that you were named after Nana, as she was beautiful, just like you. Those of you who knew her can probably easily see, in your mind's eye, her shock of white hair and her magnificent, sparkling blue eyes.

She was the youngest of seven children. She was given her name in memory of her father, Nathan, who died while her mother was still pregnant with her. The name Nathan comes from the Hebrew root that means "He gave", God gave; and we can also translate the name Natalie to "God gave". And this Natalie is the most beautiful gift that God has given us.

♦ **Bruce:** [Introduces the names "Price" and "Harder"]
Natalie's middle name, Price, is my mother's maiden name. We have given Natalie this name in honor of Walter and Naomi Price, my grandfather and grandmother who are no

longer with us. Walter and Naomi were the embodiment of lifelong partnership of husband and wife. Naomi supported Walter in his professional academic achievements, which were many, and as they grew older, Walter became Naomi's eyes as her own sight faded. Walter, who we all knew as Pop Walt, endeavored to live a meaningful life long after Naomi's passing. He was providing counsel in his deep, thoughtful voice well into his nineties. We hope that Natalie will share Pop Walt's and Grandma Price's love of life, learning, family and others in her own special way.

Natalie's last name, Harder, has a long history. Natalie is part of a very large third generation of Swiss immigrants. My grandfather immigrated to America as a young man to start a new life. My grandmother joined him and together they raised five boys on a small farm through the depths of the depression. My grandfather was a short, powerfully built man with a twinkle in his eye. He could be a joker at times. In addition to being a farmer, he was a craftsman with wood, constantly creating toys, games, and other keepsakes. My grandmother was the firm hand that kept the family in line. She was a religious person who always found a way to provide something to others who might be in need. While she became a U.S. citizen, she never lost touch with her homeland, and never missed the opportunity to share stories about life in Switzerland. She was the keeper of the oral family history. Together, Grandpa and Grandma Harder instilled a legacy built on the importance of hard work, heritage, God and family. We hope that Natalie will share in this legacy; again, in her own special way.

- ♦ **Grandma Laura:** Introduces the name "Nechama"
- ♦ **Grandpa Hersch:** Introduces the name "Faige"
- ♦ **The Gift of Tzedakah**

- ♦ **Rabbi Sisenwine:**
Beloved God, cause the parents to rejoice in this child whom you have entrusted to their care. As she has been brought into the Covenant of the Jewish People, so may she be led to the study of Torah, to enter into a marriage worthy of your blessing if this is her wish, and to live a life enriched with good deeds.

- ♦ **Ava:** [introduces *Kiddush*]
Today we drink from this cup. We first drank from it at our wedding. Our beloved friend, Karen, who is no longer with us, gave it to us for our wedding. We remember Karen today. Today, this cup is filled with the new wine of a life just begun. In it, we taste the sweetness of the joy this child has brought us. Grandpa Hersch chants *Kiddish*

- ♦ **Rabbi Sisenwine:**
May the One who blessed our mothers Sarah, Rivkah, Rachel and Leah, also bless this child and keep her from all harm. May her parents rear her to dedicate her life in faithfulness. May her heart be receptive always to Torah and Mitzvot. Then shall she bring blessing to her parents, her people, and to all the world. And let us say together, AMEN!

- ♦ **Grandpa Hersch and Rabbi Sisenwine** alternate chanting and speaking the priestly blessing.

- ♦ **Group Reading:**
"A Blessing"… (Danny Siegel in *Between Dust and Dance*)

- ♦ **All** *Shehecheyanu* and *Siman Tov u'Mazal Tov!*

In בראשית
The Beginning

SUGGESTED READING LIST

For adults

Abramowitz, Yosef I. and Silverman, Susan. *Jewish Family and Life.* Golden Books, 1997.
> A how-to book, but more. It intersperses wonderfully personal stories of family experiences along with explanations of traditions and holidays.

Diamant, Anita with Kushner, Karen. *How To Be a Jewish Parent: A Practical Handbook for Family Life*, Schocken Books, 2000. www.schocken.com.
> A unique guide to Jewish family life. Diamant provides helpful insights for parents with kids from birth to eighteen and everything in between.

Diamant, Anita. *The New Jewish Baby Book.*, Jewish Lights Publishing, 1994.
> Another gem from Anita Diamant. This book tells you everything you want to know about Jewish baby ceremonies, including naming, covenant rituals, and help for interfaith couples.

Fuchs-Kreimer, Nancy. *Parenting as a Spiritual Journey.* Jewish Lights Publishing, 1996.
> A delightful book about making sacred occasions from the everyday with your child. It will take you from 4am to getting dressed to nap time to story time to 4am.

King, Andrea. *If I'm Jewish and You're Christian, What Are the Kids?* UAHC Press, 1993.
> This is an accessible, sensitive and informational book that comes to answer many often-asked questions.

Mogel, Wendy. *The Blessing of a Skinned Knee.* Scribner, 2001.
> A thoughtful book that relates how to raise a good kid, not just how to raise a kid to feel good. Mogel speaks of many down-to-earth values that will enable your child to become a Mensch. This is advertised as great for the Jewish parent, great for the Presbyterian parent, the Buddhist, and even the skeptic.

Patz, Naomi and Perman, Jane. *In the Beginning: The New Jewish Baby Book.* UAHC Press, 1983.
> A lovely baby book for documenting all the "firsts," along with wonderful illustrations and meaningful inscriptions.

Perelson, Ruth. *An Invitation to Shabbat.* UAHC Press, 1997.
> A helpful, accessible and easy beginners guide.

Reuben, Steven Carr. *Raising Jewish Children In a Contemporary World.* Prima, 1992.
  This is an easy-to-read book that addresses many pertinent issues.

Syme, Daniel B. *The Jewish Home.* UAHC Press, 1988.
  A great step-by-step for Shabbat, the holidays, and beyond. It is clearly written
  and easily followed.

Wolpe, David J. Teaching Your Chyildren About God: A Modern Jewish Approach.
HarperPerennial, 1993.

<u>For children</u>

Abraham, Michelle Shapiro. *Good Morning, Boker Tov.* UAHC Press, 2002.
  With warm, cheerful illustrations by Selina Alko and a text that speaks to the real
  world of young children, *Good Morning, Boker Tov* helps families learn to
  transform those precious sleepy mornings into wonder-filled Jewish celebrations.

Abraham, Michelle Shapiro. *Good Night, Lilah Tov.* UAHC Press, 2002.
  A companion to *Good Morning* and also illustrated by Selina Alko, this lovely
  book helps give voice to our feelings of thankfulness and wonder and transforms
  even bedtime into a Jewish time of reflection and connection. A CD companion
  for both books is listed under music.

Brichto, Mira Pollack. *The God Around Us: A Child's Garden of Prayer*, 1999 and
The God Around Us: Unending Wonder, 2001. UAHC Press.
  Recommended highly for very young children.

Kushner, Lawrence and Karen. *Because Nothing Looks Like God.* Jewish Lights
Publishing, 2000.
  A delightful book for young children, explaining "where God is," "what God
  looks like," and "how God makes things happen." These three topics also appear
  in three board books for young children. The illustrations are equally lovely.

Rouss. Sylvia. *Sammy Spider's First Hanukah*, 1993, *Sammy Spider's First Passover*,
1995, *Sammy Spider's First Purim*, 2000, *Sammy Spider's First Rosh Hashanah*, 1996,
Sammy Spider's First Shabbat, 1998, *Sammy Spider's First Tu B'Shevat*, 2000. All from
Kar-Ben Copies, Inc.
  This great series is fun and educational at the same time.

Sasso, Sandy Eisenberg. *In God's Name.* Jewish Lights Publishing, 1994.
  This is a modern fable about the search for God's Name. It celebrates diversity
  and, at the same time, the unity of all the people of the world.

Swartz, Nancy Sohn. *In Our Image.* Jewish Lights Publishing, 1998.
   A playful new twist to the Genesis story. This book celebrates the
   interconnectedness of nature and all living things.

The Children of America. *The 11th Commandment.* Jewish Lights Publishing, 1996.
   In this inspiring book children reveal through words and pictures how they hear
   and live God's words.

Topek, Susan Remick. *A Turn for Noah.* Kar-Ben Copies, Inc.
   Other excellent titles by the same author include: *A Costume for Noah: A Purim
   Story, A Taste for Noah, Ten Good Rules,* and *A Holiday for Noah.*

Board books
Gold-Vukson, Marji. *The Colors of My Jewish Year.* Illustrated by Madeline Wikler,
Forewords Publishing, 1998.

Kress. Camille. *Let There Be Lights.* UAHC Press, 1997.
   An early Chanukah primer. This is an easy read with many bright pictures

Kushner, Lawrence and Karen. *Where Is God?* Illustrated by Dawn W. Majewski.
Skylight Path Publishing, 2001.
   A gentle way for young children to explore how God is with us everyday, in every
   way. Also check out from Skylight Paths: *What Does God Look Like?* and *How
   Does God Make Things Happen?*

Sasso, Sandy Eisenberg. *What Is God's Name?* Illustrated by Phoebe Stone, Skylight
Paths Publishing, 1999.
   A true delight...must be read to your kids! See also her other books.

Topek, Susan Remick. *Shalom Shabbat: A Book for Havdalah.* Kar-ben Copies, Inc.

Wikler, Madeline. *Let's Celebrate Shabbat!* Kar-ben Copies, Inc.

Further activity programs
Parents Are Teachers Too: The PATT Program Parent Activity Guide. Women of
Reform Judaism, 1985.
   This publication is an educational tool designed to assist parents. A learning
   experience for children, as well as parents.

Sasso, Sandy Eisenberg and Schmidt, Donald. *God's Paintbrush Celebration Kit.* Jewish
Lights Publishing, 1999.
   These are beautifully illustrated activity sheets for learning, playing, and
   exploring religion.

Music

Good Morning, Good Night: Jewish Children's Songs for Daytime and Bedtime CD, Transcontinental Music, 2002.
> A musical companion to Michelle Abraham's childrens' books.

Rosenthal, Margie and Safyan, Ilene. *Where Dreams Are Born.* Sheera Recordings. (Order through UAHC Press.)
> This is a lovely collection of Jewish Lullabies.

Sleep My Child, Blue Hill Recordings. (Order through UAHC Press.)
> A soothing collection of Jewish Lullabies from various artists.

Solnik, Tanja. *A Legacy of Lullabies.* Dreamsong Recordings, 2505 7th St., Santa Monica, CA. 90405, 1-615-383-8141.
> This is beautiful and very restful!

Websites

http://www.amazon.com: A good book source.
http://www.barnesandnoble.com: A good book source.
http://www.beliefnet.com: A multi-faith and independent resource on religion, spirituality and morality.
http://www.**clickonjudaism.org**: A dynamic, liberal Jewish Website for 20- and 30somethings that has a great deal of pertinent information and opinion.
http://www.etranscon.com: A good source of tapes and CDs.
http://www.interfaithfamily.com: Full of information on raising Jewish children in an interfaith home.
http://www.karben.com/: A good source of children's books
http://www.soundswrite.com: A good source of tapes and CDs.

Ordering sources

Jewish Lights Publishing: www.jewishlights.com 1-800-962-4544
Kar-Ben Copies, Inc.: www.karben.com/ 1-800-452-7236
Skylight Paths Publishing: www.skylightpaths.com 1-800-962-4544
UAHC Press: www.uahcpress.com 1-888-489-UAHC (8242)
Women of Reform Judaism: www.rj.org/wrj/ 1-212-650-4050

In בֵּית
The Beginning

Sponsored by the UAHC-CCAR Commissions on Reform Jewish Outreach and Synagogue Affiliation.
The Union of American Hebrew Congregations (UAHC) is the umbrella organization
for more than 900 Reform congregations across North America.

This book series is special to our family. The books teach real life lessons and the joys of hockey, family, and teammates. Hockey Day is a special holiday to all of us in Minnesota. We love these books!

—*Matt and Bridget Cullen*
Three-time Stanley Cup champion

I'm a big fan of books that teach kids about hockey and more importantly about the value of accepting those who may be different and working together as a team. It's important to lead by example and treat everyone with the same respect.

—*Claude Giroux*
Captain, Philadelphia Flyers

Keep reading, keep skating, and keep making new friends. That's what life is all about.

—*Rick Nash*
Former NHL player, Boston Bruins

This book has great lessons kids everywhere! I'm so happy my good friend Ann and the American Special Hockey Association can be an inspiration for so many people!

—*Alex Ovechkin*
Captain, Washington Capitals

This book teaches real life lessons through sport, through victory and losses, and emphasizes the importance of hard work regardless of score.

—*Jocelyne Nicole Lamoureux-Davidson*
Olympic gold medalist, Team USA

A fun story that shares the love of family and hockey!

—*Corey Perry*
NHL All-Star, Dallas Stars

Like all Minnesotans, we vote yes for Hockey Day and treasure the friendships hockey gives to all players! Keep reading!

—*Phil and Sen. Karin Housley*
Hockey Hall of Famer

I might dye my beard red, white, and blue for special hockey! Special hockey rocks! Reading is important! Do it!

—*Brent Burns*
Defenseman, San Jose Sharks

It's super cool playing hockey with my friends. I love skating, meeting new friends, and cheering for the Caps! A book about hockey, the Ice Dogs, and my dream of being the Capitals announcer is a hat trick of awesomeness!

—*Ann Schaab*
Washington Ice Dogs

I love the way this book celebrates individual differences, strengths, and similarities. When children learn about themselves, others, and the world around them, that is the ultimate hat trick.

—*Aimee Jordan*
Lila's mom; advocate for people with disabilities

Hockey is more than a sport—it's a culture. And the best part of hockey's culture is that it continually brings friends together.

—*Avery Hakstol*
Daughter of NHL coach Dave and Erinn Hakstol

HOORAY
FOR
HOCKEY DAY!

JAYNE J. JONES BEEHLER

ILLUSTRATED BY CORY JONES

Whitaker Playhouse

HOORAY FOR HOCKEY DAY!

ISBN: 978-1-64123-665-2
eBook ISBN: 978-1-64123-775-8
Printed in the United States of America

© 2021 by Jayne J. Jones Beehler
www.officialadventures.org

Illustrated by Cory Jones

Whitaker House
1030 Hunt Valley Circle
New Kensington, PA 15068
www.whitakerhouse.com

1 2 3 4 5 6 7 8 9 10 11 🅆 28 27 26 25 24 23 22 21

DEDICATION

For friendships, on and off the ice.

A NOTE FROM JAYNE

The Drop the Puck Series, showcasing brothers Blaine and Cullen, continues with *Hooray for Hockey Day*. Blaine and Ann were born with Down syndrome and have special needs. Down syndrome is a genetic disorder that can cause physical growth delays, characteristic facial features, and mild to moderate intellectual disability. Blaine and Ann's speech at times can be stuttering, slurring, and repetitive.

Get ready! It's time to cheer loud and proud—Drop the Puck: *Hooray for Hockey Day!*

1

HOCKEY DAY EVE

It was a bitterly cold Hockey Day Eve in Hockeytown USA. Stanley Cup, a bulldog with a rather unusual name, sniffed the snow boots in Luke's mudroom, licking moisture from the edges.

"Look! It's Wayne Gretzky's Oilers rookie card!" exclaimed Cullen. He was like a kid in a candy store as he and Luke sorted their mile-high collections of pro hockey player cards. When Luke wasn't looking, Cullen would sneak a trade. Their other teammates were scattered around the floor, engulfed by paper and markers, creating signs for their Hockey Day concession stand.

"I think Hockey Day should be a national holiday!" Avery declared, adding yet another layer of red to her sign's lettering.

"Isn't it already? In Minnesota, at least?" Paisley asked, glancing up from her scribbling.

"No, not an *actual* holiday. But at our house, we hang our game day socks up with care, like stockings on the mantel!" Cullen laughed and reached toward Luke's pile of cards.

Luke slapped Cullen's hand away. "We should petition Capitol Hill for an *official* Hockey Day! Like Ms. Marvin taught us about," he said.

"Us kids? Doing that?" asked Paisley, with a marker hanging from her fingers.

"We burn popcorn in the concession stand," Cullen reminded them. "You think we can get Hockey Day as a holiday?"

"I love holidays! With presents! Lots of presents!" Ann snickered.

"Yeessss, lottss of presents. Plllusss nooooo school on Hockey Day!" Blaine cheered.

Ann leapt up and triumphantly began to march in place. "I vote *yes* for Hockey Day!"

"We better not quit our day jobs just yet, senators!" Avery cautioned, gesturing at the signage that covered the floor.

"Sen-a-tors? We are the Bears!" Ann corrected. "Not the senators."

"But us going to Capitol Hill? The Bears skating outside the Capitol would be cool!" Paisley said.

"Cooooooollll," echoed Blaine.

Eager to change the subject, Cullen seized the sign Blaine was working on. "What does that say?"

"Mini donuts, sushi, nachos!" Ann proudly read out loud.

"Sushi? Since when does a hockey rink concession stand have sushi?" asked Luke.

"That's a big shift from the concessions I thought we were going to offer. Where's the popcorn and hot dogs?" Paisley asked, scooting closer to help with the sign-making.

"I-I-I-I loovvee mini donuts, I'mmmm having them for Hockkkkey Dayyyy breakfassstt, llunnchh, and dinnnnnerrr!" Blaine exclaimed. The entire group of friends giggled.

"It's a holiday now! Only the best! We serve sushi!" said Ann.

"Ugh, sushi rolls mixed with smelly hockey bags," Avery groaned.

"I might throw up." Paisley pretended to gag.

"We better stick to the original list," said Luke.

"You mean high-sticking?" Ann pretended to blow a referee's whistle. Blaine joined the fun by motioning the high-sticking penalty sign.

"Ref. Rylee would be impressed," Cullen said, "but we want to sell food! Sushi doesn't make the cut."

"I wonder if Ref. Rylee and Ref. Rosee are officiating our outdoor game tomorrow?" Paisley said. "They'd better wear earmuffs under their helmets!"

"My dad said the temperature is supposed to be five below zero!" said Luke.

"That's nothing. Cold air all feels the same. What matters is we'll be on an Olympic-size sheet of outdoor ice. Best day ever!" said Cullen.

Avery laughed. "I might need three pairs of long johns and some skate heaters."

"Someone better warn Jagger Stephen! He'll need to grow a beard overnight, like his dad!" Cullen giggled.

"His dad's beard is awesome! Will it freeze?" Ann asked. The friends all giggled at the image of a beard frozen over with spikey icicles.

2

HOCKEYTOWN USA OR BUST

Hockey Day was a combined make-believe holiday and hockey camp reunion that took place in the skating haven of Hockeytown USA. From sunrise to sundown, Hockey Day brought unlimited hours of play, thrills, and joys for the teams battling for the cherished Hockey Day Trophy. Old traditions were observed and new traditions were born. And as Hockey Day's host town, Hockeytown USA had added a special hockey festival with pro players as volunteer coaches.

As the festivities drew closer, players and refs alike were ready to drop the puck.

The hotel was overflowing with all kinds of ice-related odds and ends. "You couldn't squeeze another hockey bag in this place," Ref.

Rosee joked with the front desk clerk, smiling. "This town sure lives up to its name!" She and Ref. Rylee carefully wove their way through scattered hockey sticks, bags, and crowds of young players finding their hotel rooms.

Jagger Stephen and McLaren, along with their teammates, poured out of their team vans. McLaren instantly buried his face in his gloves. Jagger Stephen gasped and started choking on the bitterly cold air. "Are we in Minnesota or Antarctica?" he said with a chuckle.

"Now this is what I call cold!" McLaren's dad howled.

Jagger Stephen laughed as he read his first text from Cullen: "Don't stick your tongue to a metal pole! See you at the rink!"

Before they'd made it into the hotel, the team all stopped in their tracks. A sign had caught their attention: "No hockey in the hotel halls after 11 pm."

"Rockin' Rangers! We can play floor hockey at this hotel!" Jagger Stephen cheered.

"Team, we have arrived in Hockeytown USA!" McLaren shouted as the players took a picture of the sign.

"The town with more goal lights than stoplights!" added Jagger Stephen.

The team huddled around their coach as he announced room assignments and handed out the keys. "There's no running, shouting, roughhousing, or horseplay," he reminded them. "You must wear your team warm-up for breakfast, which is at 6:00 a.m. sharp."

"Six a.m.?" McLaren asked, incredulous.

The team moaned.

"We're here for Hockey Day, not playing cribbage in the lobby!" the coach responded. "And lights out by 10:00 p.m.," he added. When more moans echoed, the coach crossed his arms and tilted his head. "We can pack up our hockey bags and head home right now."

NO HOCKEY AFTER 11 PM
THANK YOU

"Ten p.m. sounds great!" McLaren grinned. As the teams

17

broke up, he turned to Jagger Stephen. "What time does the pool close? Think we still have a shot?"

"Grab your trunks," ordered Jagger Stephen. "Be in the pool in five minutes."

The swimming pool was packed. "Who's game for a belly flop contest?" McLaren called to the dozens of kids bobbing in the water.

Hands rose across the pool. "Meeeeeee!" a young boy with a bright smile exclaimed.

The boy instantly climbed out of the pool. McLaren and Jagger Stephen couldn't help but stare at him.

"Rock, paper, scissors to see who goes first?" he invited. "I might only have one leg, but it's a strong one!" He tensed the muscles in his single lower limb for emphasis. The other ended in a stump just above where the knee should have been.

"I'm Aiden," he added by way of introduction. "Some people call me Chop Chop, because I'm fast and a foodie!"

"I-I'm McLaren," he bashfully responded.

"What team?" Aiden asked.

"Team?"

"Your hockey team? You know, Hockey Day?" Another boy teased.

"He plays for the Junior Rangers with us," Jagger Stephen jumped in.

"Cool! I play for the Washington Ice Dogs," Aiden answered. Then, without warning, he squatted and dove into the pool—a picture-perfect belly flop.

McLaren and Jagger Stephen looked at each other. "He skates?" Jagger Stephen quietly asked.

"Probably better than you," McLaren replied.

"Magnificent, Chop Chop!" Jagger Stephen yelled at Aiden with a thumbs-up.

"Of course I skate!" Aiden shouted back. "Who doesn't skate in Hockeytown USA?"

"Well, then, we'll see you at the rink!" Jagger Stephen shouted.

"See you at the rink!" Aiden answered and dove back under the water.

19

3

HOCKEY DAY PERFECTION

The sunrise glowed over the two outdoor rinks, and Warroad Gardens lit up the center of the city like a beacon. Hockeytown USA had never looked better. Television crews busily set up satellites to capture all the games.

"Do you smell that?" Ref. Rylee asked Ref. Rosee, sniffing the air as they strode across one of the sheets of ice.

"Smell it? We live it!" said Ref. Rosee, throwing her arms wide to encompass the whole arena.

"Every rink has its own smell. I could walk in and pick out the Gardens without even opening my eyes!" Rylee inhaled deeply.

22

"I think maybe you've been refereeing too much hockey lately," Rosee said, chuckling.

"No, it's true. I could win big on a game show—Smell That Rink!" Rylee took another deep breath.

"Look!" Rosee said, pointing forward. "Here's the Officials' Locker Room!"

"Luke, did you take Stanley Cup out?" his dad asked.

"He won't go outside!" Luke yelled back, stuffing equipment into his hockey bag.

"What? Why?"

"It's too cold for him!"

"We have to be at the rink in twenty minutes! Get that bulldog outside!"

Luke sighed and turned to the bulldog, who had been staring with deep concern at the falling snow outside. "Listen buddy, you need to go outside," Luke reasoned with his pet. "When we leave for Hockey Day, I'll leave the TV on. You can watch us and hockey all day!"

Stanley Cup wagged his stubby tail, tilted his head, and barked.

"Boy, oh boy! We gave you the right name from the start, Stanley Cup!" Luke said, patting him on the head.

"Cullen! Cullen! It'sssss Hockeeey Daaay!" Blaine cheered.

"I'm so fired up!" Cullen replied, stuffing the last of his gear into his bag.

"Meeee toooo!"

"Two days of just hockey. You're going to be busy!" He swept the bag up onto his shoulder.

"Between being our team manager, playing for the Bears, and helping in the concession stand, you should pack a sleeping bag and just stay overnight at the rink!"

"Yeessssss! I-I-I-I shouldddddd!" Blaine high-fived his brother.

"No overnights at the rink!" their mom said, laughing.

"I-I-I-I-I could sleeeppp and showerrr in the locker room. Cooooolll," Blaine said, attempting to persuade her.

Their mom shook her head, smiling. "Boys, in the car in five minutes—without sleeping bags!"

"A little higher on the right side," Cullen instructed Avery, who arched her tiptoes even further up as she struggled with the sign and a roll of tape.

"Nice of you to finally show up," Paisley said, tapping her watch. She shifted the concession-stand signs she was holding, careful not to drop them on the already mud-stained floor.

Luke peeked into the roasters of nacho meat. "Wow! This concession stand sure is fancy." He leaned in closer. "I'm sure the food will be tasty—"

"No freebies!" Avery barked, pushing Luke's nose away.

Concessions
Mini Donuts: $2
~~Sushi: 5$~~
Nachos: 2$

"I hope we sell out of e-v-e-r-y-t-h-i-n-g! And raise a lot of loot for the special hockey and the Bears!" Paisley cheered.

"I love volunteering," Avery said, slapping a final piece of tape onto the corner of her sign. "And working the concession stand is so much fun!"

"Meeee too!! Minniiii donuts for evvverryyoone!" exclaimed Blaine.

"Don't forget, your first job is scoring back-to-back hat tricks on the ice, Avery!" said Cullen.

"Sheeeeee willlll!" Blaine high-fived Avery.

Ann and her mom arrived to work the first shift. "Where's the sushi?" Ann asked, sliding behind the counter.

"Dooooon't worry! Weeee gooottt miinnnii donnuttts!" Blaine informed her.

"Holy hockey breezers!" Jagger Stephen crowed.

"Now this is what I call a hockey palace!" McLaren said, staring at the outdoor rinks as the two boys and their teammates filed into the specially designed Hockey Day Campus.

"Look at those snow sculptures!" Jagger Stephen said, pointing into the distance.

"That's the Stanley Cup! And that's a mini replica of the Mount State of Hockey!" McLaren shouted.

"This is so cool," Jagger Stephen exclaimed, taking pictures like a tourist. The town really did live and breathe hockey.

Everyone had arrived for Hockey Day!

4

HOCKEY DAY BATTLES

Hockey Day's first match pitted friends against friends, with Hockeytown USA playing the Junior Rangers.

"Team, we have a double header. Our game is live on State of Hockey television!" Cullen said, pumping up his teammates.

"This is no time for crashing into the boards, tripping on our own blue line, or missing the net," Luke added.

"This is our rink. Our house. We play big for Hockeytown USA all day!" Avery cheered. The teammates came together in a huddle and raised their fists.

"We play every shift. Champions play every shift," said Cullen.

"We stay out of the penalty box," said Paisley.

"We work hard. Skate hard. Shoot hard," said Luke.

"We play as a team—everyone matters. Every play matters," Avery said.

"Onnnn threeee!" Blaine concluded.

"Hockeytown USA!" the entire team hollered, charging out of the locker room.

"This is unbelievable," Jagger Stephen said to McLaren as the Junior Rangers lined up.

Fans and reporters crowded around the outdoor ice rink.

"I won't need any skate warmers. The energy here is like an outdoor furnace. This place is on fire!" McLaren roared.

Ref. Rylee opened the rink door. He gave the official approval for the teams to enter the ice.

"I wish I had a helmet cam!" Jagger Stephen shouted.

"To capture all my goals against you?" Cullen asked from the center line.

"Good one," Jagger Stephen said, rolling his eyes.

After the warm-ups ended, Ref. Rylee and Ref. Rosee gathered at center ice.

The stadium speakers played the national anthem, and the teams were introduced.

"I've never seen hockey hair like that before," said Jagger Stephen, looking quizzically at the other team's disheveled heads.

"Maybe the town's barber population is equal to its stoplights," McLaren joked.

"Hockeytown USA is the crown jewel of hockey hair," Cullen stated as he positioned himself for the first faceoff. "We'll see who's laughing once the game is over."

"Sticks down, heads up," Ref. Rosee said, dropping the puck.

Ann counted on her fingers. "Five dollars, please!" she said.

"That's correct, Ann! Great job!" her mom exclaimed. The customer gave Ann a twenty-dollar bill.

Ann whispered to her mom, "She gets ten dollars back?"

"Twenty minus five is…?" Ann's mom prompted.

"I know. I know. I can do it," Ann whispered again.

"Take your time," her mom encouraged.

Ann tilted her head to the side for a moment. "Fifteen!"

The customer smiled. "I'll make you a deal. Why don't you just give me five dollars back? You can keep the other ten dollars for the Minnesota Bears!"

"Wow! That's awesome! Special hockey is sweet. I like playing. I want to be captain of my team," Ann said joyfully.

"That's terrific! I'm glad you play for the Bears—you'd make a great captain," the customer said with a wink.

"Yes, I would!" Ann said with a big smile. Her mom nudged her. "What?" Ann whispered, confused. Her mom gave her a clarifying look. "Oh yeah!" She turned back to the customer. "Thank you! My teammates will be happy! You're nice!"

"You are too!"

"You did an excellent job, Ann!" her mom reassured her as the customer walked away.

Ann sighed. "I don't like math."

"You just added and subtracted in seconds. Playing for the Minnesota Bears is giving you stamina on and off the ice!"

"What is sta-min-a?" Ann questioned.

"Stamina! It means your attention span is increasing and getting sharper. You've improved in your math skills and your homework. Plus, you can play longer on the ice without needing a break!"

"That's cool. I still don't like math. I love hockey! When I grow up, I'm going to be the announcer for the Washington Capitals! I know every player and number. That's my kind of math!" Ann declared.

"Those are my kind of goals!" her mom replied.

"I can't believe we're going to a shoot-out in game one!" Ref. Rylee exclaimed. "Pee Wee hockey at its best!"

After three regulation periods and one sudden-death overtime, the game remained tied at 6-6. Scoring the goals for Hockeytown USA were Avery, Luke, and Cullen, who had two goals each.

For the Junior Rangers, both McLaren and Jagger Stephen had hat tricks.

Cullen had managed to stay out of the penalty box, but Paisley had received a ten-minute penalty for slamming her stick against the boards.

"Each team selects three players for the first round of the shoot-out. If there's no winner, we'll proceed to round two!" Ref. Rylee explained to the teams' captains.

For the first round of the shoot-out, Hockeytown USA selected Luke, Cullen, and Avery. For the Junior Rangers, McLaren and Jagger Stephen made the cut along with a defenseman.

"Let'ssss wwwwinnnn and ffffinish thissss! Myyyy handsssss are ffffrozennnn," Blaine cheered after refilling the team's water bottles.

All six skaters scored in the first round of the shoot-out. "In round two, we play sudden death. First team that scores wins!" Ref. Rosee told the captains. "We will flip a coin to see who shoots first."

"I call heads," Jagger Stephen said.

After a few moments, Ref. Rosee announced, "Tails it is!"

Hockeytown USA selected Avery as their first shooter. As Avery began to skate forward, her left skate got caught in a large rut on the outdoor ice, and she instantly fell toward the ice. But on her way down, she made sure to get in one shot.

Her teammates were sad to see the shot fall short.

McLaren then skated to center ice and took a deep breath. He powered forward, rifled a slap shot, and scored.

Hockeytown USA had lost their first game.

5

GRAB THOSE SKATES AND GO

"The Minnesota Bears and Washington Ice Dogs play next on rink number two," announced Luke's dad. "You're up, guys!"

"Every time you get the puck, will you pass to me?" Ann asked Blaine.

"Onnlllyy ifff youuuu taaake a shottt!" Blaine quickly answered as his mom helped him lace up his skates.

"Can we fill our water bottles with hot cocoa to stay warm?" Ann suggested to her mom.

"Yesss! And marshhhhhhmellows!" Blaine added.

Ann's mom smiled. "Well, that could make them awfully sticky, but I'll see what I can do."

Blaine leaned toward her and whispered, "I'mmmmmm neerrrvvous."

"We are here to have fun, make new friends, and play hockey," Ann's mom replied, handing Ann her water bottle and helmet. "No need to be nervous!"

"Let's go Bears!" Ann cheered.

Together, the teammates marched onto the ice. After a long, straight glide, Blaine wiped out on the outdoor ice.

"Get up, Blaine! We can't score any goals sitting down!" Ann rallied.

"Oh, yes you can!" Aiden yelled as he whizzed by the duo.

"Whooooaa, loookkkk," Blaine said, pointing. Ann quickly found her mom in the crowd and waved her arms to make sure that she saw Aiden too.

Aiden was skating on ice sledge hockey equipment, racing around the rink faster than any other players. The metal frame underneath him zoomed across the ice, propelled by two sticks that the boy expertly wielded.

"Cooooollllll," Blaine said in awe, before struggling to his feet.

Hockeytown USA teammates joined the Junior Rangers on the bleachers for the special hockey festival. In special hockey games, there are no icings or offsides. Slap shots are not allowed. A whistle is blown, and a face-off occurs as volunteer referees dictate. Play is non-checking and only incidental contact is allowed. Goalies are encouraged to keep the puck in play.

"Oh my gosh! I think Aiden is faster than Cullen," Paisley roared as she scooted over to make room for Avery.

"Paging Hockeytown USA Ice Patrol! We have a speed skater on rink two, and his name's not Cullen!" Avery joked.

"Wooo-hooo, Chop Chop!" Jagger Stephen yelled. "Look at him go!"

While the other special hockey players continued to warm up, Aiden dashed across the ice at faster and faster speeds.

"I'd love to see a showdown between Chop Chop and Cullen," McLaren suggested.

"My money's on Chop Chop," Luke said.

"Mine too!" agreed Cullen, laughing.

"Go Ann! Go Blaine!" Paisley and Avery cheered and clapped.

"Dad! Dad! Up here!" Jagger Stephen called, trying to catch his dad on video. His dad looked up from among the Ice Dogs' players gathered on the team bench.

"Now, ladies and gents, my money is on the Minnesota Bears!" Avery high-fived Paisley, then turned to the bench to watch their dads, ready to coach.

"This is hockey at its best," McLaren said, shaking his head. "Even better than all of our dads' pro games combined. Right here, right now, seeing them coach these special teams—" His voice cracked, and he quickly wiped a tear that had welled up in his eye.

"Hockey is truly a game for everyone," Luke said.

"You got that right!" Paisley banged the boards, encouraging Blaine.

"Missing the shoot-out goal today and then throwing a tantrum in the locker room would seem ridiculous and minimal for this game," Avery observed. "It's the playing that matters."

The teammates and friends watched every minute, cheering for both teams and applauding their remarkable skills, talent, and persistence.

"Dad! Coach! Dad! Coach!" Avery and Paisley yelled together while pointing down the ice. "Blaine, as the cherry picker!"

The coaches jumped onto the team's bench and bellowed to the players, "Go!"

Ann passed the puck, nearly missing Aiden's stick blade. A drop pass to Blaine, it was spot-on. Its recipient was perfectly positioned as a cherry picker in front of the Ice Dogs' net.

Goal! The game was tied.

"Listen, Ice Dogs, we got this! I'll even dye my beard red, white, and blue tonight if you win this one for us," Jagger Stephen's dad said. "That's a promise."

"Don't you worry, Coach! I got our backs—I'll shoot it right through the pipes!" Aiden said with a grin.

And just like that, Chop Chop hustled, skating from the farthest corner of the rink to its opposite, coast to coast. With a smack he shot the puck into the net, scoring the game-winning goal.

"What a snipe!" Jagger Stephen's dad shouted to McLaren's dad, clapping him on the back. "Special hockey rocks!"

"Yes it does! A great win and even better players!" McLaren's dad said.

"Race you to get mini donuts!" Ann challenged Blaine as she unlaced the last of her gear.

"Yummmmmm!" Blaine responded, running out of locker room.

6

HOCKEY DAY BREAKAWAYS

"The concession stand is cleaned and ready for tomorrow's games!" Ann's mom announced.

"I loved it! I loved collecting money!" Ann winked.

"Anddddd tassttttyyy work!" Blaine added.

"We sold a lot of hot dogs and mini donuts! We raised major money for special hockey!" Paisley exclaimed as she helped Avery count the stand's money.

"Hi there!" Jagger Stephen said, walking up to the stand. He pulled some crumpled bills from his pocket. "I'll take eight bags of mini donuts please."

"Eight—eight bags?" Ann asked.

"It's my dad's lucky number. Eight bags of mini donuts will bring eight sweet, hot goals tomorrow!" Jagger Stephen smiled.

"You'd better start eating more than just eight! Try eighty-eight!" Cullen joked.

"Weeeeee arreee clossssed," Blaine interjected.

"Closed?" Jagger Stephen whined.

"But we'll still take your money—you said eighty-eight bags?" Avery asked with a big grin.

"We were going to bring them back to the hotel—to share with Aiden and the Ice Dogs," McLaren said.

"Cool," said Ann.

"Fuuuuunnn," Blaine said, rubbing his stomach.

"Even Blaine can't eat eight bags of mini donuts!" Paisley said.

"Yeessss I cannn," Blaine replied.

"We love that idea! Here's a few leftover goodies from today that you can share," Ann's mom offered.

"Yes! Thank you!" Jagger Stephen answered.

McLaren took the box of treats.

"Sounds like a party to me!" Avery said, dancing.

"Holy cow, you guys," exclaimed Luke from the side. "For real? We made $3,088 today!"

"Woooowwww!" Blaine cheered, spinning around.

"Too cool for hockey school," Cullen said.

After officiating five games, Ref. Rylee joined Ref. Rosee in the hotel lobby. "A well-spent Hockey Day!" The two high-fived.

"Incredible competition, joyful players, and stellar sportsmanship," Rosee summarized the day.

"That's a hat trick!" Rylee said, laughing and dodging a foam puck. "You can take the hockey players out of the rink, but you can't take the hockey out of the players."

The hotel lobby and pool area quickly became a makeshift floor hockey rink. Players from the Ice Dogs and Junior Rangers played hallway floor hockey and card games and laughed until just shy of their coach's curfew.

Just as things were starting to wind down, Jagger Stephen's dad entered the lobby. As he stepped out of the shadows into the light, the players couldn't help but notice that something was *different* about his appearance.

"Whoa!" Jagger Stephen exclaimed, grabbing his phone.

Aiden just looked on, gaping.

Ref. Rosee couldn't control her laughter.

"Is that permanent?" asked McLaren.

"Taking Hockey Day to the extreme, eh?" asked Rylee.

"Red, white, and blue! Just like my team ordered!" Jagger Stephen's dad smiled, stroking his colorful beard. The mop of hair had gone from dull brown to a vivid three-color rainbow.

"Don't move, Dad! This will go viral in seconds!" Jagger Stephen ordered, stepping closer to get a better angle for his video.

"A deal is a deal, right, Aiden?" asked his Hockey Day coach.

Aiden pointed his finger at his coach and asked, "Can I tug on it?"

"Bhaaaaaaa," the coach replied, jostling Aiden. The entire hotel lobby erupted in laughter.

"Wildest beard on Hockey Day! That's one amazing coach," Rosee said.

As the hockey game in the lobby continued, friendships became the top-shelf breakaway on this Hockey Day.

7

HOCKEY DAY, THE HOLIDAY

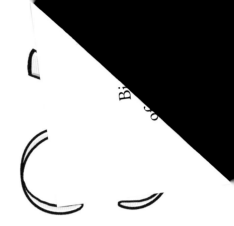

Months had passed since Hockey Day, and the piles of snow were beginning to melt. Hockeytown USA had wrapped up their winning season. Moms and dads were beginning to make their kids' annual summer plans.

Cullen, Luke, Jagger Stephen, and McLaren were heading back for another month-long adventure at Minnesota Hockey Camps. Avery and Paisley were excited to join Coach Lamoureux in Detroit Lakes for a girls' hockey school of champions, teaming up to teach Learn to Skate lessons all summer.

Ann and Blaine had decided to stay close to home with weekly summer practices for the Minnesota Bears. The dazzling duo, along with Aiden, were going to be busy all summer, modeling for an upcoming hockey equipment ad.

ggest of all in everyone's minds, however, was a different kind
hockey celebration.

"Culleeennn! Cuulllllleenn!" Blaine yelled loudly.

Cullen woke suddenly, rolled over in his hotel bed, and looked
at his brother.

"What?" he asked, stretching himself upright.

Blaine was standing in front of the room's mirror, looking at the
neon-orange bow tie twisted around his neck.

"Here, lil' bro," Cullen said, reaching over and correctly
fastening the bow tie.

"IIIIIIII loooookkkk handsome," Blaine proudly proclaimed.

"Minus a few wrinkles in your shirt," Cullen punched back,
straightening the shirt and holding his brother's shoulder.

"Bigggggg ddayy," Blaine said.

"Every day is a big day with you. I love you, Blaine," Cullen said,
ruffling his brother's hair.

"Boys, you ready to go? Your teammates are sitting in the lobby waiting!" their dad called from the adjoining room.

"Holy breezers and frozen hockey pucks," Avery mumbled, taking pictures of the governor's office.

"I think 'Senator Luke' has a nice ring to it," Luke told his team as they took a seat on the governor's couch.

"Not as nice of a ring as 'Governor Paisley,'" Avery shot back, high-fiving Paisley.

"I'll be too busy playing for Team USA in the Olympics to run a political campaign," Cullen countered. The team giggled, a sound that abruptly ended when a young man in a suit strode into the room.

"The governor is ready for the proclamation signing. Please follow me," stated the young assistant.

The team and their parents slowly walked into the governor's press room. Paisley took a deep breath. Avery's mouth dropped at the sight of the antique chandelier. Blaine grabbed his mom's hand after seeing the line-up of television cameras ready to film the announcement.

The governor, after the usual waving and shaking of hands, moved to the microphone. "Every day is a great day for hockey. I thank these young players for writing to me and asking for Hockey Day to be recognized as an official Minnesota holiday. Minnesota is the State of Hockey. Hockey is for everyone, and today we are making it official," stated the governor as he signed the proclamation.

The press began to ask questions.

"Cullen? What does Hockey Day mean to you?" a reporter asked.

Cullen smiled and looked at his brother. "Seeing my little brother play hockey and knowing hockey *really is* for everyone."

"Ann? What does Hockey Day mean to you?" asked another reporter.

Ann looked at her mom. "Go ahead, Ann," her mom encouraged.

"I love hockey. I love my friends more. I want to be my team's captain next year, and when I grow up, I want to be the announcer for Hockey Day!" Ann said, beaming.

"Hired!" the governor interjected.

"To me, hockey is awesome and means friendship," Aiden typed on his computer to Jagger Stephen and McLaren.

"Right back at ya, buddy," Jagger Stephen typed.

McLaren closed the livestream and said, "Super cool to watch the proclamation signing with Chop Chop. Hockey friendships are the best!"

"Yep," Jagger Stephen agreed. "Hooray for Hockey Day!"

STATE of MINESOTA

Proclamation

HOCKEY DAY

Governor

ASK THE OFFICIALS
RYLEE AND ROSEE'S REFEREE RESOURCES

Important Words to Learn

Antarctica: Earth's southernmost continent and site of the South Pole

Cherry picking: Loafing or floating in ice hockey; the floater (a player) literally casually skates behind the opposing team's defenseman

Etiquette: Code of polite behavior

Governor: The elected executive or head of state

Ice sledge hockey: A special kind of hockey that allows players with disabilities to compete;

players use metal frames to move across the ice

Persistence: continuing an action even when it is difficult or discouraging

Petition: A formal written request

Proclamation: Special recognition issued by the governor or other government official for extraordinary state or local events

Rut: A deep crack in the ice

Sudden death: A rule in a competition where the game ends immediately when one team gains a lead over the other; traditionally has been used in hockey playoff and championship games

Warroad Gardens: A 70,000-square-feet square arena featuring an Olympic-size ice sheet, eight locker rooms, and 1,454 theater-style seats, located in Warroad, Minnesota (Hockeytown USA)

MEET JAYNE

Jayne J. Jones Beehler wears many helmets, including hockey sister, college professor, lawyer, author, wife, mother, advocate for children with disabilities, and lifelong hockey fan. She's also a former live-in nanny who can never have enough children or chaos around her. Jayne resides in Florida with her husband, a hockey coach and former goalie. Every night, there's a game on their TV! Together, they founded a chaperone travel nonprofit organization to ensure that individuals with developmental disabilities can travel independently.

www.officialadventures.org

OTHER BOOKS IN THIS SERIES!

AVAILABLE WHEREVER
CHILDREN'S BOOKS ARE SOLD!